Historical Information for New Testament Students

by JOHN BLIGH

HELICON · BALTIMORE

HELICON PRESS INC.
1120 N. Calvert Street, Baltimore, Md 21202

This edition first published 1967

BS
2410
B6
1967

Imprimatur: ✠ Josephus F. Cleary
              Vicarius Capitularis
              Romae: 5a Oct. 1965

Printed in Great Britain

The field of New Testament study is not confined to the brief period of Christ's ministry, death and resurrection (c. A.D. 27–30). It includes the years covered by the Acts of the Apostles (A.D. 30–63), the period during which the books of the New Testament were written and collected (A.D. 45–100), and the period in which the New Testament canon was stabilized (c. A.D. 140–200).

At the other end, the period cannot begin with the year 27, or even with 5/4 B.C. (the probable date of the birth of Christ). In order to understand the political and religious situation into which Christ was born and within which he conducted his ministry, one must go back at least to 167, the beginning of the Maccabean Wars.

The period covered by New Testament study, therefore, runs from 170 B.C. to A.D. 200. It begins with Judaism tightly shut in upon itself; it ends with Christianity separated off from Judaism, and propagated far and wide throughout the Roman Empire.

From the point of view of world history, what Christ achieved in his brief ministry was *the founding of the Church*, which has been an important power in the world ever since. From this point of view, the field of New Testament study can be described as 'Christian Beginnings'. Its main sources are the books of the New Testament, but these should not be studied in isolation. The other literature of the period often casts valuable light on the main sources.

This collection of HINTS contains the background material which an able student can reasonably be expected to carry in his memory. It has therefore been kept brief; detail which is hard to remember has been deliberately omitted. When the reader has mastered the contents of this book, he should fill out his knowledge by reading some of the fine volumes listed in the bibliography on p. 118. The authors of these represent a variety of Christian denominations or traditions. On matters of history, fortunately, we are rarely in disagreement. May the day come quickly when our other differences will be resolved.

References are occasionally given in footnotes to articles and books which will be found of particular value. It is not intended that these references be committed to memory.

CONTENTS

1. Jewish Writers in Greek

PHILO of Alexandria, born about 25 B.C., a member of a rich and powerful family, became a philosopher and Scripture scholar.[1] He writes for Jews of the Greek Diaspora who are in daily contact with the high civilization of the Hellenistic world and who may be tempted to think that the wisdom of the Greek philosophers outshines the revelation contained in the Bible. By means of allegorical interpretations, he attempts to show that Greek wisdom is contained in the Bible and may even be derived from the Bible. For example, in his treatise *Who is the heir?* (214), he claims that Moses anticipated Heracleitus's doctrine of opposites. Two treatises which are useful for comparison with the Epistle to the Galatians are *Who is the heir?* (for St Paul too discusses who are the heirs of Abraham), and *The Preliminary Studies*, in which Philo allegorizes Sarah and Agar. (Both are in Vol. IV of the Loeb translation of Philo.)

In A.D. 39, Philo represented the Jews of Alexandria on an embassy to Rome. He has left an account of it in a treatise called *The Embassy to Gaius*. He died within a few years.

Flavius JOSEPHUS, born in A.D. 37 of a noble and priestly family, became a Pharisee. In the Jewish war of 66–70, he led the Jewish resistance in Galilee. After performing wondrous feats of valour (so he tells us), he was captured by the Romans and brought to Vespasian. Claiming the gift of prophecy, he ingratiated himself by foretelling that Vespasian would become emperor. He was liberated and took Vespasian's family name Flavius as a mark of gratitude. In *c.* A.D. 75, he was in Rome, where he wrote *The Wars of the Jews* in seven books, a work of propaganda, to deter his

[1] Cf. H. Chadwick, 'St Paul and Philo of Alexandria,' *Bulletin of the John Rylands Library*, 48 (1966), 286–307.

fellow Jews from further revolt. In the reign of Domitian he wrote his *Antiquities of the Jews* in twenty books, to enhance the prestige of the Jewish people in the eyes of the Graeco-Roman world. It was published in A.D. 93. He also wrote a *Life* of himself, to refute the charge that he had caused the revolt of 66, and a treatise *Against Apion*, an Alexandrian who had written an attack on the Jewish religion.

2. Codifications of Jewish Tradition

At the time of the destruction of Jerusalem (A.D. 70), a disciple of Hillel named Rabbi Johannan ben Zakkai gathered the surviving Pharisaic teachers at Jamnia. He opposed the policy of armed revolt from Rome and discouraged the apocalyptic fervour of the Zealots. He developed a sober form of Pharisaism concentrating on what the Law requires a man to *do* here and now.

At Jamnia, Johannan and his associates began the process of codifying the oral traditions of the Pharisees. For a time, each teacher could make his own compilation or MISHNAH (a word meaning 'repetition' or 'second law'), but eventually the Mishnah of Rabbi Judah ha-Nasi (who died in A.D. 220) became the only one used in the schools. The Mishnah as we have it is a revision of the work of Rabbi Judah. A complete English translation is available: H. Danby, *The Mishnah*, Oxford, 1933—a book of 844 pages.

The two TALMUDS are commentaries on the Mishnah. They give the Mishnah, section by section, with the 'Gemara' or expansion and comment. The so-called 'Jerusalem Talmud' was first issued at Tiberias about A.D. 250. The Babylonian Talmud appeared about 400. Both continued to grow by the addition of further comments during the next two centuries. Here is a specimen passage from the Babylonian Talmud, Sanhedrin, 43a, which casts light on Mark 15: 23.

What of R. Hiyya ben Ashi's dictum in R. Hisda's name:

When one is led to execution, he is given a goblet of wine containing a grain of frankincense, in order to benumb his senses, for it is written: *Give strong drink unto him that is ready to perish, and wine unto the bitter of soul* (Prov. 31 : 6). And it has also been taught: The noble women of Jerusalem used to donate and bring it. If these did not donate it, who provided it?—As for that, it is certainly logical that it should be provided out of the public funds: since it is written *Give*, the implication is of what is theirs.

3. Pagan Writers

Cornelius TACITUS, A.D. *c.* 55–*c.* 125, became proconsul of Asia. His chief works are the *Annals* and the *Histories* describing imperial times. Of less importance, but worthy of mention, is his *Life of Agricola*, his father-in-law, who commanded the Roman forces in Britain under the Flavian emperors. A brilliant stylist, he created many immortal phrases, such as *omnium consensu capax imperii, nisi imperasset* (of Galba).

Gaius SUETONIUS Tranquillus, A.D. *c.* 69–*c.* 140, was a member of the equestrian order. For a time he was secretary to the emperor Hadrian. In 121 he published a collection of *Lives of the Caesars* from Julius Caesar to Domitian.

PLINY the Elder, A.D. *c.*24–79, was killed by going too close to Vesuvius when it was erupting in 79. He may have been on the staff of Titus during the Jewish War. His sole extant work is his lengthy *Natural History*.

PLINY the Younger, nephew of Pliny the Elder, A.D. *c.* 61 to *c.* 114, left a large collection of Letters written or rewritten for publication. Letters X, 96–97 are of particular interest—a correspondence between Pliny, then governor of Bithynia, and the emperor Trajan, about the persecution of Christians.

4. The Earliest Extant History of the Church

EUSEBIUS, the 'father of Church history', was born at Caesarea about A.D. 260. He was a friend of Constantine, the first Christian emperor, who put an end to the age of persecutions by the so-called 'Edict of Milan' in A.D. 313. At Constantine's side, Eusebius played a leading part in the Council of Nicaea of A.D. 325, which condemned Arianism and defined the homoousion. His greatest work is his *History of the Church from Christ to Constantine*. It contains many valuable fragments of earlier Christian writers whose works are now lost.

Test

Write your answers to these twenty questions on a piece of paper.

Who was the rabbi who gathered the Pharisees at Jamnia?............1

In what year did Philo go on his embassy to Gaius?..................2

When was Josephus born?.................................3

Which was written first, the Talmud or the Mishnah?..............4

Name an Epistle in which St Paul discusses who are the heirs
of Abraham...5

Where was the 'Jerusalem Talmud' produced?..................6

What type of exegesis did Philo mostly employ?.................7

The present Mishnah is a revision of the work of whom?..........8

What was Josephus's second great work?....................9

What was the name of Tacitus's father-in-law?..............10

What ancient writer was killed by the eruption of Vesuvius?.....11

Where was Philo born?.................................12

Who was the first Christian emperor?......................13

Who wrote the *Lives of the Caesars*?....................14

From which emperor did the younger Pliny receive a letter
about the persecution of Christians?....................15

Where was Pliny at the time?...........................16

Who is called 'the father of Church history'?..............17

When did the Council of Nicaea take place?................18

When did the Babylonian Talmud appear?..................19

Of whom was the phrase *capax imperii* first used?..........20

Now check your answers by re-reading the text.

From the beginning of the second century B.C., the Holy Land was subject to the Seleucid kings of Syria. In 167 B.C. King Antiochus Epiphanes decided to destroy the Jewish religion and force the Jews to hellenize (i.e. to adopt the Greek way of life). His aim was to create religious and cultural uniformity throughout his multi-racial empire.

In pursuance of this policy, he visited Jerusalem, set up a statue of Olympian Zeus (the chief god of the Greeks) in the temple, sacrificed swine, and forbade circumcision. These measures provoked the Jews to rebellion.

The Jews were led by a certain Mattathias, of the family of Hasmon. He had five sons, the third of whom, named Judas, was given the title 'Maccabaeus' (which probably means 'the Hammer'). During this war, the Jews entered into alliance with the Romans, but Roman troops took no part in the fighting. The temple was re-dedicated in 164. In memory of this event, the Jews annually celebrated a feast called 'Dedication' or 'Encaenia'. It is mentioned in John 10.

The war was fought in defence of the Law and of the religion of the Law. The Jews won, partly because Syrian forces were needed elsewhere. Their victory was a victory for the Law. Hence the result was an accentuation of the distinction between the Jews and their pagan neighbours. The Law became more than ever a wall of separation.

The first and second Books of Maccabees cover the same events and are not by the same author. The first was written about 145 B.C.; the second is a digest, made in about 75 B.C., of a much longer history by Jason of Cyrene, who wrote about 125 B.C.

From 142 to 63 B.C., the Jews enjoyed a period of independence under the Hasmoneans, who supplied both kings and high priests. In 63, Pompey deposed the last Seleucid king and annexed Syria to the Roman empire. He besieged and captured Jerusalem, and offended the Jews by inspecting the Holy of Holies.

Test

QQ. 13–20 are repetition questions. The numbers in brackets refer to the page on which the answer can be found.

In 63 B.C., when Pompey intervened in Jewish history, two Hasmonean princes were contending for the throne: Hyrcanus and Aristobulus. Pompey chose Hyrcanus as ruler, but gave him only the title 'high priest', not 'king'; for what had been the Hasmonean kingdom was now attached to the province of Syria.

Under Hyrcanus there rose to power, as general and chief minister, an Idumean named Antipater. Herod was his son. (Idumea in the south of Palestine had been annexed by the Maccabeans, and its inhabitants had been forcibly converted to Judaism. For this reason Herod's enemies were able to call him a half-Jew.)

In 47, Julius Caesar separated the Holy Land from Syria. He made Hyrcanus ethnarch, Antipater procurator of Judaea, and Herod governor of Galilee.

In 43, Antipater was poisoned. Herod stepped into his position as procurator, and became betrothed to Mariamne, who was a granddaughter of Hyrcanus and thus a Hasmonean princess. Herod loved this arrogant woman passionately, but she hated him.

In 40, the Parthians invaded Syria and entered Palestine with a Hasmonean pretender named Antigonus. Herod fled to Rome, where he won the favour of Mark Antony and Octavian (later called Augustus), who directed the senate to proclaim him King of the Jews. With the aid of two Roman legions he conquered his kingdom in 37. Antigonus was sent to Antioch, where Antony had him executed. In this year 37, Herod married Mariamne. She gave him two sons, Alexander and Aristobulus, whom he eventually sent to Rome for their education. In 29 B.C. he was persuaded to have Mariamne executed. Till this date he was monogamous; afterwards he went to pieces and had nine wives.

8

Herod was confirmed in his kingdom by Augustus, during whose reign he made two further visits to Rome, one to bring back the two sons of Mariamne, and the other to seek Augustus' permission to put them to death. However, Augustus effected a reconciliation. A later request for the same permission (in 7 B.C.) was granted. Augustus remarked that it was better to be Herod's pig than his son.

Herod was a great builder. He rebuilt Caesarea with an artificial harbour which remained one of the chief ports of the Levant till the Middle Ages. In 20 B.C., he began the rebuilding of the temple on the scale of the temple of Solomon. But he also built three pagan temples in the Holy Land, one at Caesarea, one at Sebaste (his new city in Samaria), and one at Panias (later called Caesarea Philippi), not to mention several in Gentile lands.

He died a loathsome death, from cancer of the bowels, at Jericho in 4 B.C., five days after executing another of his sons.

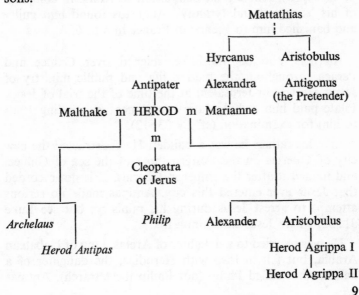

In his will Herod divided his kingdom, subject to the approval of Augustus, among three of his sons. He assigned

to Archelaus: Idumaea, Judaea, and Samaria;

to Antipas: Galilee and Peraea;

to Philip: Gaulanitis, Ituraea, and Trachonitis.

The will was contested in Rome, but Augustus confirmed it. He gave Archelaus the title of 'ethnarch' and the other two the title of 'tetrarch' (but their subjects seem to have ignored these distinctions and called them kings).

ARCHELAUS, son of Malthake, reigned from 4 B.C. to A.D. 6. When the Holy Family returned from Egypt, hearing that Archelaus was king of Judaea, Joseph was afraid to settle there and withdrew to Galilee (Mt 2: 22). In A.D. 5 the Jews and Samaritans, despite their mutual hostility (see p. 45 below), sent a joint deputation to Rome to complain of his 'savagery and tyranny'. Augustus found him guilty and banished him to Vienne in France in A.D. 6.

ANTIPAS, son of Malthake, reigned over Galilee and Peraea throughout the hidden life and public ministry of Jesus. He was in Jerusalem at the time of the trial of Jesus. Pilate paid him a diplomatic compliment by sending Jesus to him for examination (cf. Lk 23: 12).

Like his father, he was a builder. He constructed the new city of Tiberias on the western shore of the sea of Galilee, and named it after the emperor Tiberius. It is not recorded that Jesus ever entered this city. Antipas made no serious attempt to arrest Jesus during his ministry; but see Luke 31: 32, where Jesus calls him a fox.

He was married to a daughter of Aretas, king of Nabatean Arabia, but fell in love with Herodias, the daughter of a half-brother called Philip (not Philip the tetrarch). Antipas divorced his wife, Herodias divorced her husband, and they married. (Salome the dancer was Herodias's daughter by her previous marriage.) John the Baptist was imprisoned and executed for condemning this marriage. Later Aretas made war on Antipas and severely defeated him.

In A.D. 39 Herodias persuaded Antipas to go to Rome and ask the emperor (Caligula) for the title of king. But Herod Agrippa (I) accused him of plotting revolt, and he was banished to France. Herodias voluntarily went with him to share his exile.

PHILIP, son of Cleopatra of Jerusalem, married Salome, the daughter of Herodias. He alone of the sons of Herod is praised by Josephus. He rebuilt Bethsaida, which he named 'Julias', and Panias, which he named 'Caesarea Philippi' (he added 'Philippi' to distinguish his Caesarea from the one rebuilt by his father on the coast).

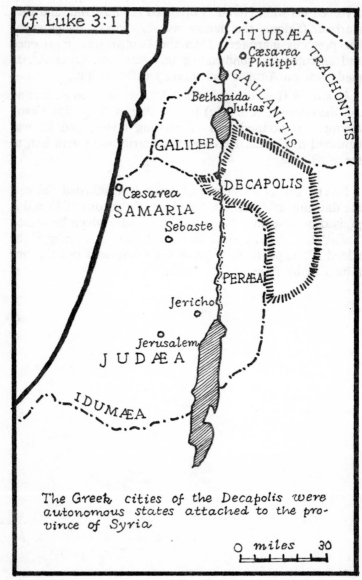

Cf. Luke 3:1

ITURÆA
TRACHONITIS
Cæsarea
Philippi
GAULANITIS
Bethsaida
Julias
GALILEE
DECAPOLIS
Cæsarea
SAMARIA
Sebaste
PERÆA
Jericho
Jerusalem
JUDÆA
IDUMÆA

The Greek cities of the Decapolis were
autonomous states attached to the province of Syria

0   miles   30

Whom did Pompey appoint high priest in 63 B.C. ? 1

What was the name of Herod's father? 2

What office did Julius Caesar give to Herod? 3

To what great family did Mariamne belong? 4

When did Herod marry her? 5

When did he put her to death? 6

In what year did the Parthians invade Palestine? 7

What were the names of the sons of Mariamne? 8

In what year were they put to death? 9

Who was the mother of Archelaus and Antipas? 10

Who was the mother of Philip the tetrarch? 11

In what city did Herod build a harbour and a pagan temple? 12

When did he begin to rebuild the temple at Jerusalem? 13

In what year did Herod die? 14

What is the probable date of Christ's birth? (v) 15

Who reigned over Galilee during the public ministry? 16

Who rebuilt Bethsaida and Panias? 17

What was the name of the Nabatean king who defeated Antipas? 18

Over what regions did Archelaus rule? 19

Before which Herod did Christ appear during his trial? 20

THE JULIO-CLAUDIAN EMPERORS

The Roman emperors from Augustus to Nero all belonged to two great families, the Julii and the Claudii, which were linked by the marriage of Augustus and Livia. Not one of these emperors was succeeded by a son of his own.

Augustus	B.C. 27–14 A.D.	41 years	⎫
Tiberius	14–37	23	⎪
Gaius (Caligula)	37–41	4	⎬ 95 years
Claudius	41–54	13	⎪
Nero	54–68	14	⎭

During this period, the principate was not in theory an hereditary monarchy. Theoretically, each emperor was chosen by the senate and people. Constitutionally, the power which he held was (*a*) tribunician power (*potestas tribunicia*), which was primarily civil power, and (*b*) proconsular power (*imperium proconsulare*), which was primarily military. The senate continued to appoint consuls year by year, and often the emperors would take this office for a year. But the consular power was no longer supreme.

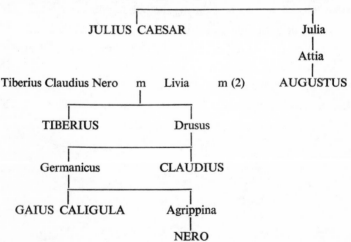

14

AUGUSTUS was a grandson of Julius Caesar's sister, Julia. Julius Caesar adopted him as son and heir. His first great achievement was to put an end to the Roman civil wars by knocking out all his powerful rivals. Together with Antony, he defeated Brutus and Cassius at Philippi in 42 B.C.; then in 31 B.C. he defeated Antony at Actium. In 27 B.C. he became the first emperor, with the title *princeps*, but he was always careful to preserve the appearances of republican government.

He reorganized and consolidated the frontiers along the Rhine and Danube, and inaugurated a period of peace such as the Mediterranean world had not known for centuries. In this peace Christ was born.

He reorganized the administration by creating an imperial civil service, and put taxation on a businesslike basis by carrying out censuses in the provinces. The census of Luke 2 was a small part of this policy.

He permitted and even encouraged emperor-worship in the eastern provinces (where emperor-worship and king-worship were traditional) as a means of unifying the subject peoples and fostering loyalty to Rome. But he did not impose such worship upon the Jews.

He liked Herod the Great, kept him in office, and after his death confirmed his will. But after deposing Archelaus in A.D. 6, he put in Roman procurators to govern Judaea.

TIBERIUS was the son of Livia by her first marriage, and thus a stepson of Augustus. He was an able general and administrator, and was notoriously severe in punishing provincial governors who misused their power. He was an unamiable character, and eventually retired to the island of Capri and ruled the empire from there. But Tacitus has painted him in darker colours than he deserved.

He appointed Pilate as procurator of Judaea in A.D. 26 and left him in office until 36—which implies that Pilate's

15

administration met with his approval. The whole of Christ's brief ministry was carried out in the reign of Tiberius. When Jesus was shown the coin of the tribute, the image and inscription were probably those of Tiberius—unless it was an old coin left over from the time of Augustus.

Tiberius allowed divine honours to be paid to the deified Augustus, but restrained those who wished to pay them to himself. In this he contrasts with his successor.

GAIUS, known as 'CALIGULA' or 'Little Boots', a nickname given him by legionaries when he was a boy, was the grandson of Tiberius's brother Drusus.

Probably he was a little mad. He not only permitted but demanded that divine honours be paid to himself. When the governor of Egypt attempted to set up cult-images of him in the synagogues of Alexandria, the Jews of that city sent an embassy to Rome under Philo. While Philo was in Rome, Gaius ordered Petronius, the governor of Syria, to set up his statue in the temple at Jerusalem. Petronius, realizing that he could do this only over the dead bodies of countless Jews, declined to obey. Gaius sent an order for him to commit suicide, but before this reached Petronius, he had received news from other messengers that Gaius had been assassinated by officers of the Praetorian Guard in Rome, who had been alienated by his increasingly despotic rule. (The Praetorian Guard was the garrison of Rome and the emperor's bodyguard.)

Gaius tried and condemned both Pilate (in 37) and Herod Antipas (in 39).

CLAUDIUS was Caligula's uncle. As a child he had been unhealthy and rather neglected. When unexpectedly made emperor, he showed equally unexpected ability. He expanded the imperial bureaucracy, and added Britain to the Roman empire. In an attack on Colchester, he used elephants.

16

During his reign occurred the widespread famine prophesied by Agabus (Acts 11). In about 49 he issued an edict banishing Jews from Rome, in consequence of which St Paul met Aquila and Priscilla in Corinth. The edict is mentioned by Suetonius in his Life of Claudius, where he says that the Jews had been constantly rioting at the instigation of one 'Chrestus'. This may mean that the arrival of Christianity split the Jewish community in Rome and led to riots.

In Judaea, Claudius interrupted the series of procurators in A.D. 41, when he made (Herod) Agrippa I king of Judaea. But the extravagance of Agrippa and the revolt of Theudas in 44 showed that it was preferable to have a Roman governor. After the death of Agrippa in 44, procurators were appointed again.

St Paul's first two missionary journeys belong to the reign of Claudius. Gallio, the governor of Achaea, before whom St Paul appeared in 51–2 or 52–3, owed his appointment to Claudius. Gallio was the elder brother of the philosopher Seneca, who was to rise to influence at the court of Nero.

NERO was nephew of Caligula and adopted son of Caligula's uncle and successor, Claudius. For the first five years he governed well, but absolute power corrupted him. Believing himself a great artist, in A.D. 66 he made a tour of Greece, entered for musical competitions at the festivals, and, not surprisingly, won many prizes.

When St Paul appealed to 'Caesar', he was appealing to Nero, and to Nero he was sent. After being bitten by a Maltese snake, he arrived in Rome in A.D. 61, and remained in prison for two years awaiting trial. Whether he was at last tried, and if so with what outcome, Acts does not narrate. About this time, St Peter too arrived in Rome. The two apostles suffered martyrdom at Rome under Nero, perhaps in 64, but more probably in about 67.

17

The persecution of 64 was the result of a fire which devastated part of Rome in that year. Nero was suspected of arson, probably wrongly. To provide a scapegoat, he held the Christians responsible and killed them with horrible ingenuity. He may be the Beast of the Apocalypse; 666 is a gematria for 'Nero Caesar' (i.e. the numerical equivalents of the consonants of 'Neron Caesar' in Hebrew add up to 666).

During his reign, the procurators of Judaea tried the patience of the Jews too far, and war broke out in 66. Nero appointed Vespasian to be governor of Syria and quell the rebellion with the legions from Syria. (In Britain, Boadicea rebelled and was defeated in A.D. 60.)

Nero died by suicide in A.D. 68.

THE YEAR OF THE FOUR EMPERORS—In Nero the Julio-Claudian dynasty died out. After this, the weakness of the Roman empire revealed itself: any ambitious general could turn his legions towards Rome and make a bid for the principate. In the year 68–69, four generals did this: Galba, Otho, Vitellius, and Vespasian.

What was the name of Tiberius's mother?..1

How long did the Julio-Claudian dynasty last?....................................2

Whom did Octavian (later Augustus) defeat at Philippi?.................3

In what year did he defeat Antony at Actium?....................................4

Who appointed Pilate procurator of Judaea?.......................................5

What relation was Gaius to Claudius?...6

Who appointed Gallio governor of Achaea?...7

When did St Paul appear before Gallio?...8

Who was Gallio's more famous brother?..9

Who reigned first, Gaius or Claudius?...10

Which emperor tried to have his statue set up in the temple
   at Jerusalem?..11

Who was the governor of Syria who refused to obey?.......................12

In what year did Claudius banish the Jews from Rome?..................13

By whom was Gaius assassinated?..14

In what years was Herod Agrippa I king of the Jews?....................15

Who was the father of Herod Agrippa I? (9) 16

In what year did Nero tour Greece?..17

In what year did the Jewish War begin?...18

The four emperors of 68–69 were Galba, Otho, who, and
   who? 19

As in Latin DIX=509, so in Hebrew NRN QSR=666;
   what is such an equation called?..20

When Archelaus was deposed in A.D. 6 his territory was not made into a Roman province but was loosely joined to the province of Syria. It was placed under a governor who had the title of 'procurator' and was subject to the supervision of the governor of Syria (always a senior general, of senatorial rank, with the title 'legate of Augustus'). Ordinarily the procurator of Judaea acted independently, but in extraordinary circumstances the governor of Syria had the right and duty to intervene.

The procurators were not nobles of senatorial rank, but members of the equestrian order or 'knights'. They came from families of successful business men. The first procurator of Judaea was Coponius, A.D. 6–9. Josephus (*Wars*, II, 8, 117) says: 'Coponius was sent out, having received from Caesar all power including power of life and death.' This is usually, and correctly, taken to mean that capital jurisdiction was reserved to the procurator (cf. Jn 18: 31). Some Jewish authors maintain that the Sanhedrin too had power to pass and execute a capital sentence; they then argue that since Jesus did not die by stoning (the Jewish method of execution), he was not even condemned by the Sanhedrin.[1] The duties of the procurators were:

1. To keep the peace and suppress rebellion. In Judaea the procurator had five auxiliary cohorts, recruited mainly from Sebaste and Caesarea. One of these was always stationed in the castle Antonia, overlooking the temple. The procurator normally resided at Caesarea, but he came up to Jerusalem for the festivals, to suppress any nationalistic rising. In A.D. 58, St Paul was rescued from a mob by soldiers who ran down from the Antonia.

---

[1] The arguments adduced in support of this position are criticized in J. Blinzler, *The Trial of Jesus*, Cork, 1959, pp. 157–63.

Lysias, the officer in command of the cohort, sent Paul under armed escort to Caesarea.

2. To administer justice in capital cases. The Sanhedrin and local courts dealt with most cases, but the right of life and death was reserved to the procurator. The procurators sentenced criminals to beating or flogging or scourging, or to the frightful death of crucifixion. They did not impose long-term prison sentences as punishments. (The Sanhedrin could inflict fines and beatings, and could order a thief or debtor to be sold into slavery.)

3. To collect taxes for the imperial treasury. The title 'procurator' refers directly to this duty. (Pilate took money from the temple treasury to pay for an aqueduct to bring water into Jerusalem; the plan was excellent, but the seizure of the money caused a riot and much bloodshed.)

PONTIUS PILATE, the fifth procurator, was appointed by Tiberius in A.D. 26 and left in office until 36. Tiberius did not believe in changing governors frequently. They were so avaricious that to change them annually was to apply a fresh blood-sucker every year. Both Philo and Josephus accuse Pilate of intolerable cruelty. In Luke 13:1 there is mention of 'Galileans whose blood Pilate mingled with their sacrifices'. In A.D. 36 he put down a riot in Samaria with such brutality that the Samaritans protested to the legate of Syria. He deposed Pilate and sent him to Rome for trial. When he arrived in Rome, Tiberius was dead. He was tried by Caligula and was probably ordered to commit suicide. (The death of Pilate became the subject of many Christian legends.)

In A.D. 41, Claudius interrupted the series of procurators and made Herod Agrippa I king of the Jews, ruling all the territories of Herod the Great. But after the death of Herod Agrippa I in 44, procurators were appointed again, and the series continued until the Jewish Revolt of A.D. 66.

Between 44 and 66 there were seven procurators. The last four were:

FELIX, who imprisoned St Paul (not as punishment, but to await trial).

FESTUS, who sent Paul to Rome. Festus died in office in 62. In the interregnum which followed, Annas (jr) put to death James the brother of the Lord.

ALBINUS, who deposed Annas for having acted *ultra vires*.

GESSIUS FLORUS, who provoked the Jews to revolt in 66.

Test

The period 175 B.C. to A.D. 200 was the formative period not only of Christianity, but also of Judaism. This period saw the rise and extinction of the Essene and Sadducean sects, and the rise of the Pharisees, whose theology and piety were to become normative for later Judaism.

Outside the Scriptures, our best source of information on the three sects is Josephus, who says in his *Life*:

> While still a mere boy, about fourteen years old, I won universal applause for my love of letters; in so much that the chief priests and leading men of the city used constantly to come to me for precise information on some particular of our laws. At about the age of sixteen, I decided to gain personal experience of the several sects into which our nation is divided. These, as I have frequently mentioned, are three in number—the first that of the Pharisees, the second that of the Sadducees, and the third that of the Essenes. I thought that after a thorough investigation, I should be in a position to select the best.

At the age of nineteen, he selected the Pharisees as the best. The above passage shows not only that Josephus had the Pharisaic vice of boastfulness, but, what is more important, that a young Jew of the higher classes could choose for himself which sect he would join, and that to join any of the sects he had to pass through a period of training. St Paul, an older contemporary of Josephus, was brought up as a Pharisee by his parents, and then trained in law, literature and theology by the Pharisee Gamaliel. Each sect had its own doctrines, its own teachers, and its own schools.

It is uncertain which sect of the Jews produced the apocalyptic literature (on which see p. 61 below)—perhaps the Essenes, perhaps the Pharisees.[1]

[1] Cf. G. E. Ladd, *Jesus and the Kingdom*, London, 1966, pp. 73–75.

24

The Sadducees probably took their name from Sadok, a high priest of the time of Solomon. This sect drew its members chiefly from the priestly families, but it included wealthy and conservative laymen too. The high-priestly family of Annas belonged to the Sadducean sect (cf. Acts 5: 17), but many of the poorer priests were Pharisees (cf. Jn 1: 19).

In the time of Christ the Sadducees were the dominant party in the Sanhedrin. They adopted a conciliatory policy towards the Roman authorities and were content to preserve the *status quo*.

Theologically, they disagreed with the Pharisess on the following points:

1. Whereas the Pharisees accepted both Scripture and tradition, the Sadducees regarded Scripture as the only source of revelation.

2. The Sadducees denied the resurrection of the body. According to Josephus, they held that the soul perishes with the body. The resurrection of Lazarus was, therefore, a great embarrassment to the Sanhedrin. The only recorded encounter between Jesus and the Sadducees during the public ministry was a debate concerning resurrection (Mt 22: 23–33). In A.D. 58 St Paul was able to split the Sanhedrin by claiming that he was on trial for defending the resurrection of the dead (cf. Acts 23).

3. In regard to divine providence and human freedom, the Pharisees emphasized God's control over human affairs, the Sadducees emphasized man's freedom.

4. The Sadducees applied literally the *lex talionis* ('an eye for an eye and a tooth for a tooth'); the Pharisees were less rigorous in imposing punishments.

The ascendancy of the Sadducees ended with the destruction of the temple in A.D. 70. After this, the Pharisees enjoyed unchallenged pre-eminence in Judaism.

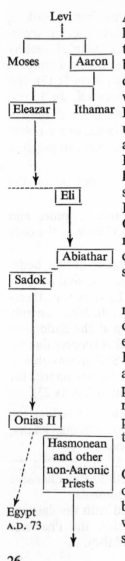

Levi

Moses — Aaron

Eleazar — Ithamar

Eli

Abiathar

Sadok

Onias II

Hasmonean and other non-Aaronic Priests

Egypt
A.D. 73

According to the Law, the high priesthood was a hereditary office, belonging to the descendants of Aaron. It was held by Aaron's son Eleazar and by his descendants down to the time of Eli, who was descended from Aaron through Ithamar; then by the descendants of Eli until in 973 Solomon deposed Abiathar and appointed Sadok, who was of Eleazar's line. The descendants of Sadok held the office in uninterrupted succession until 175 B.C., when Antiochus Epiphanes deposed Onias II. His son Onias III fled to Egypt and established a new temple at Heliopolis, where his descendants continued the high-priestly succession until A.D. 73.

From the time of Antiochus onwards, none of the high priests had any hereditary right to the office. The Hasmoneans seized it for themselves. Under the Romans the office was bought with gifts, and no one was high priest for life. In practice the high priesthood became the monopoly of a few wealthy, aristocratic priestly families, the chief of which was the house of Annas.

Annas was appointed high priest by Quirinius in A.D. 6 and retained the office until A.D. 15. Five of his sons became high priests, and Caiaphas, who was high priest from 18 to 36, was his son-in-law.

When Jesus was arrested, he was led first to Annas—a mark of deference to him as head of the high-priestly family. The formal trial of Jesus was conducted by Caiaphas. Caiaphas was deposed in A.D. 36 by Vitellius, legate of Syria, at the same time as he deposed Pilate. In the Acts of the Apostles Peter and John too are tried before Annas and Caiaphas (4: 6).

The Books of the Maccabees speak of a party called the *Hasidim* (Hebrew for 'the pious'). After the Maccabean wars, no more is heard of them. It is conjectured that the Pharisees and Essenes, who appear after the war, were re-groupings of the former Hasidim.

The Pharisees appear to have become a recognizable sect about 125 B.C. The word 'Pharisee' is usually derived from the Hebrew verb *paras*, 'to separate'. They separated themselves off from the common people, and still more from the Gentiles, by their exact observance of the Law and of their oral traditions, which, they believed, went back to Moses. (It has, however, been suggested that originally 'Pharisee' meant 'one holding Persian beliefs'.[1])

The Pharisees were for the most part laymen, though a priest could be a Pharisee if he wished. Many of the scribes were Pharisees (a 'scribe' is a man trained in the Law; each sect had its scribes). Through teaching in the synagogues they acquired great influence over the people, whose consciences they oppressed with burdensome rules and regulations, and especially with an over-strict interpretation of the sabbath law.

The Pharisees were the principal opponents of Jesus during his public ministry. He condemned both their teaching and their hypocrisy. Nowadays, there is a tendency to whitewash the Pharisees. Some of them undoubtedly were holy men with high moral ideals; and many of their sayings are memorable. But they also indulged in some minute and vexatious casuistry, e.g. as to which knots may be tied on the sabbath and which may not. And for the few who succeeded in mastering their rules, pride was almost inevitable.

[1] Cf. T. W. Manson, 'Sadducee and Pharisee,' *Bulletin of the John Rylands Library*, 22 (1938), pp. 12 ff.

At the trial of Jesus, the Sadducees were dominant in the Sanhedrin. Hence the legality of the trial ought not to be judged by the standard of the Pharisaic 'traditions' which were idealized and codified in the Mishnah.

St Paul was a Pharisee before his conversion, and may have considered himself still a Pharisee to the end of his life (cf. Acts 26: 5). Other Pharisees were converted to Christianity. Some of them remained too attached to the Law and attempted to force its observance on Gentile Christians. St Paul opposed them, and his view prevailed at the Council of Jerusalem in A.D. 49 (cf. Acts 15 and Gal. 2: 1–10).

Down to the reign of Herod the Great, the teaching tradition of the Pharisees was carried on by 'pairs' of teachers, most of whom are mere names to us, but not the last pair: Hillel and Shammai, whose period of activity coincided roughly with Herod's reign.

Hillel came to Jerusalem from Babylon, where there was still a Jewish community with schools of the Law. After studying at Jerusalem under the previous pair (Shemaiah and Abtalion), he became the greatest teacher of his day. Shammai was a native of Judaea.

The earlier pairs were not heads of conflicting schools, but Hillel and Shammai gave conflicting decisions on so many points of the Law (more than 30⁰) ⸱hat they created two schools, the 'House of Shammai' and the 'House of Hillel'. In their decisions Shammai was the stricter, Hillel the more lenient. After the fall of Jerusalem, the House of Hillel gained the ascendancy.

An important difference between the two schools concerned the grounds of divorce. The divorce law of Deuteronomy 24: 1 says that a man may dismiss his wife if he finds in her some 'uncleanness of a thing' (*'erwath dabar)*—a very vague phrase. Shammai took the strict view that it meant adultery; Hillel took the lax view that even burning the husband's food was sufficient grounds for divorce. When the Pharisees asked Jesus (Mt 19: 3): 'Can a man lawfully divorce his wife for any reason whatever?', they were inviting him to take sides in this controversy between the schools of Hillel and Shammai.

Many anecdotes were told about this pair. One is that a man went to Shammai and said: 'Teach me the whole of the Law while I stand on one foot.' Shammai, who was a carpenter, drove him away with a yardstick. He put the same question to Hillel, who said: 'Do not do to your neighbour what you hate to have done to you. That is the whole Law, entire; the rest is explanation. Go and learn.'

Hillel was much more ready to welcome proselytes than Shammai. There is a saying of Hillel: 'Be disciples of Aaron, loving peace and pursuing peace, loving mankind (i.e. all men), and drawing them to the Law.'

Test

THE ESSENES

The Essenes are described by Josephus, Philo and Pliny the Elder, but are not mentioned in the New Testament. Jesus appears to have had no contact with them. They were probably an offshoot of the Hasidim. From Josephus's description it appears that they were a monastic community, practising celibacy and holding their property in common. Pliny says that they had a settlement in the desert north of Engedi, near the Dead Sea. But according to Josephus they also had houses throughout the country for the sake of hospitality. About A.D. 50, they numbered about 4,000.

The Essenes were exact observers of the Law, but held aloof from the ritual of the temple, as they did not acknowledge either the priesthood or the official calendar of Maccabean and post-Maccabean times. They observed the sabbath so strictly that they refrained from easing their bowels on that day.

They had secret doctrines about the angels, and took a vow not to divulge their names. This led Bishop J. B. Lightfoot to suspect a link between Essenism and the doctrine attacked by St Paul in Colossians.

Pliny's description, in his *Natural History*, Book V, is as follows:

On the west (of the Dead Sea) the Essenes keep away from the shore as far as it has harmful effects, a solitary race and astonishing above all others in the world, without women-folk, without sexual intercourse, without money, the companions of palm trees. As time goes on, the assembled throng is reborn in equal numbers by the accession of numerous men weary of life, whom the waves of fortune bring to their manner of life. Thus through the course of thousands of centuries (incredible though it seems) the race is eternal though in it no one is born—so prolific for them is other men's repentance for their past lives. To the south was the town of Engedi. . . .

Josephus, in his *Wars*, Book II, says:

They have no one city, but in each they live in numbers. And for the members of the sect who come from elsewhere everything lies open just as if it belonged to them.

At Qumran, near the north-west shore of the Dead Sea, are the ruins of a monastic settlement, founded about 150 B.C. and occupied until the war of A.D. 66–70, during which it was destroyed by the Romans. This settlement is probably to be identified with the monastery of the Essenes mentioned by Pliny as situated north of Engedi.

The climate at Qumran is terrible. The Dead Sea is about 1200 feet below sea-level; the river Jordan constantly flows into it; but it has no outlet. Between three and four million tons of water evaporate off the surface daily. The Essenes chose this site in fulfilment of Isaiah 40:3: 'In the desert prepare a way for the Lord.' The community prepared a way for the Lord by studying the Law of Moses and striving to keep it perfectly. They were expecting two Messiahs, a priestly Messiah and a royal Messiah.

In A.D. 66, they sealed up their books (which were in the form of scrolls) in earthenware jars, and hid them in caves in the sandhills above the monastery, hoping to recover them after the war. Some of them remained there till 1947, when a Bedouin shepherd boy threw a stone into one of the caves and heard the smash of earthenware. When he went inside to investigate, he made the first find of the famous 'Dead Sea Scrolls'. Since then, several other finds have been made in the same neighbourhood.

One scroll is a copy of Isaiah, written about 150 B.C.— a thousand years older than any other manuscript of Isaiah. Other scrolls contain the *Manual of Discipline* or Rule Book of the community, and a collection of Thanksgiving Psalms. The *War Scroll* describes the eschatological 'War of the Sons of Light against the Sons of Darkness'. There is also a *Commentary on Habakkuk*, which attempts to show how the prophecy has been fulfilled in the life and times of the founder of the community, the 'Teacher of Righteousness'

35

The importance of these scrolls for the study of the New Testament has been greatly exaggerated. They have in fact made little difference. Here are a few points of contact.

1. Some scholars think the scrolls cast a little light on the mysterious figure of John the Baptist. He too made much of Isaiah 40: 3, and he may possibly have been a member of the Qumran community before he started preaching to the sons of darkness.

2. The community followed an unofficial calendar, according to which, in the year of the crucifixion, they ate the paschal supper on the Tuesday of Holy Week. A French scholar (Mlle Annie Jaubert) suggested that Christ too followed this calendar, and therefore his arrest took place on the Tuesday night. This would explain how according to Matthew–Mark–Luke he had eaten the paschal supper before his arrest, whereas according to John 18: 25 the chief priests on Friday morning would not enter the governor's palace in order to avoid a defilement which would have prevented them from eating the paschal supper that evening (Friday). However, the theory that Christ and his disciples followed an unofficial calendar, out of step with the liturgy of the temple, has not commended itself to the majority of scholars.

3. The Manual of Discipline (III, 13–IV, 26) contains a 'Two Spirit theology' which resembles the 'ethical dualism' of the fourth gospel, viz. the antitheses between light and darkness, life and death, truth and falsehood, above and below, sons of God and sons of the devil:

> It was He (God) who created man to rule the world and appointed two spirits by which he would walk up to the time of His visitation. These are the spirits of truth and of wickedness. In the fountain of light is the birth of truth, but from the source of darkness is the birth of wickedness. In the hand of the Prince of

Lights is the dominion of all the sons of righteousness; in the ways of light they walk. And in the hand of the Angel of Darkness is all the dominion of the sons of wickedness; and in the ways of darkness they walk. And it is through the Angel of Darkness that any of the sons of righteousness go astray. And all their sin and their iniquities and their guilt and their deeds of transgression are under his dominion according to the mysterious decree of God until his end.

There follows a description of the two ways of life in the world, which resembles the Two-Ways document incorporated in the *Didache* and *Epistle of Barnabas* (see below, pp. 81–2).

During the period of the Judges, there were temples and altars in several places (e.g. Shiloh and Nob). By the law of Deuteronomy 12: 5–7, however, the sacrificial cult was confined to one place—which, from the time of Solomon, meant the temple at Jerusalem.

Solomon's temple was destroyed by the Babylonians in 587. At this time, the Ark of the Covenant and Aaron's rod disappeared. After the return from Exile, the building of a much smaller temple was begun in 536, but the people were poor and the work lagged. Thanks to the exhortations of the prophets Haggai and Zechariah, the building was completed in 516. The Samaritans wished to share in the work of reconstruction, but their offer was rebuffed.

Herod the Great rebuilt the temple on a splendid scale, beginning in 20 B.C. (cf. Jn 2: 20). The work was completed just a few years before the destruction of the temple by Titus in A.D. 70. The Herodian temple was the first to include a court of the Gentiles, perhaps in conformity with the prophecy of Isaiah 56: 7: 'My house shall be a house of prayer for all the nations'—quoted by Jesus at the Cleansing of the Temple.

The temple was served by a hereditary priesthood, divided into twenty-four 'courses' or groups of families, which served a week at a time in rotation. Zachary, the father of John the Baptist, belonged to the course of Abiah (cf. Lk 1: 5). Every priest had to know his genealogy, to prove his right to serve. There were daily public sacrifices, morning and evening, and countless private sacrifices. On the chief festivals (Passover, Pentecost, and Tabernacles) and on the Day of Atonement, all twenty-four courses served together.

The sacrifice of the Day of Atonement was always offered by the high priest, who alone could enter the Holy of Holies (which, after the Exile, was completely empty). Apart from this, the high priest could offer the sacrifice when he chose. Usually he did so on the sabbaths, new moons and great feasts.

The Levites were originally priests of local shrines, who were deprived of their functions when Josiah in 620 B.C. enforced the prohibition of Deuteronomy against the offering of sacrifices elsewhere than at Jerusalem. The deposed clergy suffered hardship and were invited to Jerusalem, where they became priests of second rank. Deuteronomy 14: 29 makes them the object of public charity. Cf. John 1: 19.

PASSOVER (April) commemorated the Exodus from Egypt. On the 13th of the month, Nisan, all leaven was destroyed. From 14th to 21st only unleavened bread was eaten. On the 14th the paschal lamb was slain in the temple by the offerer, and its blood was thrown before the altar by a priest. The roasted lamb was eaten with bitter herbs and unleavened bread. The head of the household explained, in the Passover *Haggadah* ('Explanation'), the significance of these rites. The Hallel was sung (Pss. 113–18). All Jews tried to be in Jerusalem or its immediate neighbourhood for this great national feast.

PENTECOST (June), a week of weeks ($7 \times 7 = 49$ days) after the sabbath following Passover, was a harvest festival. The liturgical readings were from the Book of Ruth. The historical 'Creed' of Deuteronomy 26: 5–10 was recited at the offering of the first-fruits (of the barley harvest).

After the destruction of Jerusalem in A.D. 70, the rabbis treated this feast as a commemoration of the Lawgiving at Sinai, which they believed took place fifty days after the departure from Egypt. But this explanation of the feast is not to be found in Philo or Josephus.

THE DAY OF ATONEMENT (Sept./Oct.—10th of Tishri) was the day of the great sacrifice of expiation. For all Jews it was a day of rest and of fasting. The ritual is described in Leviticus 16. The scapegoat was led out into the desert. The high priest took the blood of victims into the Holy of Holies itself.

It is not recorded that Jesus was ever in Jerusalem for the Day of Atonement. In Romans 3: 25, St. Paul indicates that the death of Christ is the antitype of the sacrifice of the Day of Atonement. The contrast is elaborated in Hebrews 9.

40

TABERNACLES (Sept./Oct.—15th of Tishri) was originally the festival of the wine and oil harvests. For a week the people lived in huts or 'tabernacles' built of greenery. Palms and other branches were waved during the singing of the Hallel. The temple courts were illuminated at night, and there was a solemn libation of water (Jn 7: 37–38 may be connected with this rite).

DEDICATION (December—25th of Kislev) commemorated the re-dedication of the temple in 164 B.C. after its desecration by Antiochus Epiphanes. Josephus calls it 'the Feast of Lights'. Each evening of the week more and more lights were lit in the temple. In John 10: 22–24, during this feast, Jesus is challenged to say whether he is the Messiah.

Test

WEALTH, POVERTY, SLAVERY

In the time of Christ, there were extremes of wealth and poverty in the Holy Land. The wealth of the rich was enormous. Josephus gives the following estimates of annual income:

Archelaus	600 talents;[1]
Antipas	200 talents;
Philip	100 talents.

Hence the income of Herod the Great must have been about 1,000 talents. Herod Agrippa I is said to have received 12,000 talents. These kings, the high priests, and the chief landowners had palaces with hundreds of slaves and servants. They lived in great luxury and banqueted in the grand manner.

There was a middle class of retailers, craftsmen, innkeepers, etc. Most of the priests, who received tithes of the crops, were in this bracket, but many were poor, since tithes were evaded by some and inequitably distributed.

The greatest part of the population in Jerusalem was poor—the slaves, day-labourers, and beggars. Large numbers of beggars, blind, lame and sick, came to Jerusalem to live by the alms of the pious.

There were both Jewish and Gentile slaves in the time of Christ. A Jew could become a slave in three ways:

1. A Jew convicted of theft and unable to make restitution could be sold into slavery (cf. Mt 18: 25).

2. In extreme poverty an adult male Jew could sell himself into slavery.

3. A Jewish father could sell his daughter to a Jew. At the age of 12 she became free, and would normally become the wife of the buyer or of his son.

[1] One talent=10,000 solid silver coins the size of a half-dollar or an English florin.

A Jewish slave had to be released after six years (cf. Exod. 21: 2), but a Gentile had to serve for life. Hence Gentile slaves sold at a much higher price. In the time of Christ most of the slaves in Palestine were from Arabia, booty of the Herodian wars. There was a slave market in Jerusalem.

After the death of Solomon, the kingdom was divided in two. For the northern kingdom (Israel), a new capital was eventually built by Omri and Ahab—the city of Samaria. When it fell to the Assyrians in 722 B.C., many of its inhabitants were deported, and peoples from other lands were substituted (cf. 2 Kgs 17). After this, the Jews of Judaea regarded the Samaritans as a mongrel people.

After the return of the exiles of the southern kingdom, the Samaritans offered to take part in the rebuilding of the temple (doubtless on the understanding that they would have some control of it when finished), and were rather rudely rebuffed by Ezra (cf. Ezra 4: 2). On Mount Gerizim, which had been an Israelite holy place before Jerusalem, they built their own temple. The Jews destroyed it in 129 B.C., and in the time of Christ it lay in ruins. In about A.D. 10, the Samaritans desecrated the temple in Jerusalem shortly before the Passover by scattering bones in the temple courts. The Jews retaliated by excluding Samaritans from the temple.

The place called 'Aenon near Salim' where John the Baptist worked (cf. Jn 3: 23) was probably in Samaria, a few miles from Sychar.[1] John 4: 9 may mean that Jews did not 'use the same vessels as the Samaritans' (who were presumed to be unclean).[2] A formal regulation on this point, made in A.D. 65 or 66, probably codified an existing custom. But John 4: 9 may well have a wider meaning: 'Jews do not associate with Samaritans.'

Jesus did not share the hostility of his fellow Jews to the

[1] Cf. W. F. Albright, 'New Discoveries in Palestine and the Gospel of St John', in *The Background of the New Testament and its Eschatology* (Studies in honour of C. H. Dodd), Cambridge, 1956, p. 159.

[2] Cf. D. Daube, 'Jesus and the Samaritan Woman: the meaning of *synchraomai*', *Journal of Biblical Literature*, 69 (1950), pp. 137–147.

Samaritans, as can be seen from the parable of the Good Samaritan and from John 4.

The gospel was preached in Samaria by Philip the deacon, who converted Simon Magus. The Samaritan converts were then visited by Peter and John, who confirmed them (cf. Acts 8: 4–17). According to some of the Fathers, Simon Magus was the first Christian Gnostic. Another Gnostic heresiarch, Dositheus, certainly came from Samaria.

About A.D. 100, Justin Martyr was born in Samaria. He became prominent as a defender of the Christian faith, and addressed one of his two 'Apologies' to the emperor Antoninus Pius. Justin's principal work is his *Dialogue with the Jew Trypho*.

'Diaspora' is a Greek word meaning 'dispersion'. The Jews regarded dispersion as a divine punishment for their disobediences and looked forward to the 'gathering in' of all Israel as one of the blessings of the Messianic era.

The dispersion can be regarded as beginning with the deportation of 50,000 exiles to Babylon by Nabuchadnezzar. There were also deportations to Egypt, and large numbers of Jews emigrated voluntarily, for economic reasons, to Arabia, Armenia, Persia, etc.

In the time of Christ, there were more Jews living in the Diaspora than in the land of Israel. The Jewish community of Alexandria in Egypt was estimated by Philo at 1,000,000. Over 150 cities of the Roman empire are known to have had synagogues in the time of Christ.

The 'Septuagint', a Greek translation of the Hebrew Scriptures, was made at Alexandria in the third and second centuries B.C., for use in the liturgy of the Greek Diaspora. The legend of how it was made by seventy (Latin *septuaginta*) translators, who worked separately but all produced exactly the same version, is told in the so-called *Letter of Aristeas*.

The synagogues of the Diaspora attracted large numbers of proselytes and still larger numbers of 'God-fearers' (the *phoboumenoi*). These were men who observed the Jewish food laws and attended the synagogue meetings, but shrank from the final step of circumcision.

The synagogues of the Diaspora paved the way for the Christian missions. When St Paul entered a Greek city, he always began by preaching in the synagogue, if there was one. Probably many of his best converts were drawn from among the God-fearers. This would explain the hostility which his synagogue-preaching frequently provoked: he was creaming off the best of their Gentile sympathizers.

47

Test

48

THE SYNAGOGUES

The word 'synagogue' can mean either the *building* in which a community of Jewish men meet for prayer and study of the Law, or the *meeting* of Jews at such a building.

The synagogues probably came into existence as a result of the concentration of sacrificial worship in Jerusalem. Outlying communities still needed a local centre of religious practice. But the synagogues became important during and after the Exile. When the temple was destroyed and the sacrifices ceased, the Law or Torah became the centre of the religion of Israel. After the return from Exile, the synagogues and the Bible were not eclipsed by the rebuilt temple and its sacrifices. From that time on, the religion of the Jews has been the religion of the Book.

While the temple was controlled by the priests, the synagogues were controlled by laymen. Each had at least one 'ruler of the synagogue', and an 'attendant' who looked after the scrolls of the Law.

Prayers were offered in the synagogues morning and evening at the time of the sacrifices in Jerusalem. On the sabbath there were regular readings from the Law and the Prophets (probably according to a three-year cycle), and these were followed by a sermon given by a scribe or by any competent layman. Jesus, who was of course a layman (not of the tribe of Levi), often preached in the synagogues, but very little of his synagogue preaching has been preserved.

As the Hebrew text of the Old Testament was not understood by the ordinary people, after a passage of Scripture had been read in Hebrew, a translation was given in the vernacular Aramaic. At the time of Christ, the translator had to give his Targum ('translation') by heart. The Scripture was written and had to be read even if known by heart; the Targum was oral and had to be given by heart.[1] Often

[1] Cf. B. Gerhardsson, *Memory and Manuscript*, Uppsala, 1961, p. 68.

the Targum was a free translation, with a measure of interpretation added. The writing down of the Targums began in the first century A.D. A manuscript of the Jerusalem Targum of the Pentateuch was discovered in the Vatican Library in 1957 (it had been catalogued under an incorrect title) and will be published soon. It will give us the Aramaic version used in Palestine in the time of Christ.

It is to be regretted that we do not possess the prayer books used in the synagogue-liturgy of Christ's day, for we do not hear that he found fault with them. However, scholars have reconstructed the 'Eighteen Benedictions' which, it is believed, were in daily use in Christ's time. About A.D. 85 the Pharisees at Jamnia inserted the *Birkath ha-Minim* (a curse upon Christians and heretics)—which meant that thereafter Christians could not take part in the Jewish synagogue liturgy. Here is the text:

1. Blessed art Thou, O Lord, God of Abraham, God of Isaac and God of Jacob, God most High, who art the Possessor of heaven and earth, our Shield and the Shield of our fathers. Blessed art Thou, O Lord, the Shield of Abraham.

2. Thou art mighty, strong, that livest for ever, that raisest the dead, that sustainest the living, that quickenest the dead. Blessed art Thou, O Lord, that quickenest the dead.

3. Holy art Thou and Thy Name is to be feared, and there is no God beside Thee. Blessed art Thou, O Lord, and holy God.

4. O favour us, our Father, with knowledge from Thyself and understanding and discernment from Thy Torah. Blessed art Thou, O Lord, who vouchsafest knowledge.

5. Cause us to return, O Lord, unto Thee, and let us return anew (in repentance) in our days as in the former time. Blessed art Thou, O Lord, who delightest in repentance.

6. Forgive us, our Father, for we have sinned against Thee; blot out and cause our transgressions to pass from before Thine eyes. Blessed art Thou, O Lord, who dost abundantly forgive.

7. Look upon afflictions and plead our cause, and redeem us for the sake of Thy Name. Blessed art Thou, O Lord, the Redeemer of Israel.

8. Heal us, O Lord, our God, from the pain of our heart, and cause Thou to rise up healing for our wounds. Blessed art Thou, O Lord, who healest the sick of Thy people Israel.

9. Bless for us, O Lord our God, this year and satisfy the world from the treasuries of Thy goodness. Blessed art Thou O Lord, who blessest the year.

10. Blow the great horn for our liberation and lift a banner to gather our exiles. Blessed art Thou, O Lord, who gatherest the dispersed of Thy people Israel.

11. Restore our judges as at the first, and our counsellors as at the beginning; and reign Thou over us, Thou alone. Blessed art Thou, O Lord, who lovest judgment.

12. For apostates let there be no hope, and the dominion of arrogance (=Rome) do Thou speedily root out.

    And let Christians and minim perish in a moment, let them be blotted out of the book of the living, and let them not be written with the righteous.

13. Towards the righteous proselytes may Thy tender mercies be stirred, and bestow a good reward upon us together with those that do Thy will. Blessed art Thou, O Lord, the trust of the righteous.

14. Be merciful, O Lord our God, towards Jerusalem, Thy city, and towards Zion, the abiding place of Thy glory, and towards the kingdom of the house of David, Thy righteous anointed one. Blessed art Thou, O Lord, God of David, the Builder of Jerusalem.

15. Hear, O Lord our God, the sound of our prayer, for a God gracious and merciful art Thou. Blessed art Thou, O Lord, who hearest prayer.

16. Accept us, O Lord our God, and dwell in Zion; and may Thy servants serve Thee in Jerusalem. Blessed art Thou, O Lord, whom in reverent fear we serve.

17. We give thanks to Thee, who art the Lord our God, for all the good things, the steadfast love which Thou hast shown to us. Blessed art Thou, O Lord, unto whom it is good to give thanks.

18. Bestow Thy peace upon Israel Thy people and bless us, all of us together. Blessed art Thou, O Lord, who makest peace.[1]

---

[1] Cf. W. Förster, *Palestinian Judaism in New Testament Times*, London, 1964, p. 157.

Judaism in Christ's day was not homogeneous, but it is possible to generalize and form some idea of the beliefs held by most of his hearers when he preached in the synagogues and in the temple (cf. Jn 18: 20).

About the Structure of the Universe

The ordinary people no doubt accepted the pre-scientific (or 'mythological') cosmology presupposed in the Old Testament.

1. The earth is a flat disc floating on water ('the waters under the earth').
2. The sky is a solid firmament. Over it are 'the waters above the earth'.
3. God dwells with his court of angels high above the firmament. (The Biblical phrase 'the heaven of heavens' had given rise to the picture of a three-decker division within heaven; hence St Paul's reference to 'the third heaven' in 2 Cor. 12: 2.)
4. The demons inhabit the lower air.
5. It is not clear how far the Jews still accepted the old picture of She'ol as a place where the dead lead a pale, unsatisfying, unenviable existence.

As nothing was known about the expansion and contraction of gases, the movement of the winds was a mystery (cf. Jn 3: 8). As nothing was known of light rays, sight was believed to beam out of the eye, and mirrors were a mystery. Darkness was regarded as something black, not simply as the absence of light.

54

About Angels and Demons

From the beginning of biblical history, God has a court of angels, who adore him and serve him as ministers and messengers (*angelos* is the Greek for 'messenger'). In the mind of the individual Israelite, they enhanced the majesty and transcendence of God.

In the intertestamental literature (Jubilees, Enoch, The Testaments of the Twelve Patriarchs, Fourth Ezra, the Dead Sea Scrolls) the angels figure more prominently. They are divided into groups and given names. They guard individuals and may appear in human form (like Raphael in the Book of Tobias).

In Matthew 18: 10, Christ seems to take for granted that his hearers already believe that each individual has a guardian angel.

In the intertestamental period there is also a great development of demonology (perhaps a retrograde development[1]). The Jews believed that the earth was infested by legions of evil spirits (causes of temptation, sin, and sickness), organized under a fallen angel, Satan, or Beelzebub, or Belial. Christ performed many exorcisms, and saw his passion as a conflict with 'the ruler of this world' (Jn 12: 31).

About Man

Beliefs about man were based on Genesis 1–3: man was created by God to rule over the beasts of the earth. God looked on him and saw that he was good; but through the external influence of the devil he was corrupted (cf. Wis. 2: 24). Death took hold of him, making him morally weak even while he lives, and therefore unable to hold out against temptation. But it was not doubted that with God's aid Israel *could* keep the Law, if sinners would repent.

[1] Cf. G. von Rad, *Old Testament Theology*, II, Edinburgh, 1965, p. 349.

The Greek distinction between a material body and a purely spiritual soul was not part of the popular religion. The 'soul' was probably thought of as a thin material wraith, which escapes at death. Hence survival was pictured as the resurrection of the body, not as the immortality of a purely spiritual soul. (Here the Wisdom of Solomon, written in Greek, is exceptional: the author looks forward to a blessed life, probably in the Greek form of immortality.)

Belief in resurrection of the body was a late development. Job 7: 9 and Isaiah 38: 18 say that from She'ol there is no returning. Probably reflection on the deaths of the Maccabean martyrs first stimulated belief in resurrection: it was felt that for such men death could not be the end; they would rise to share in the Good Time Coming. The first clear evidence of this new belief is Daniel 12: 2–3 and 2 Maccabees 7: 9. The fate of men who had sinned and had then died fighting for the Law presented a problem; some drew the conclusion that it is a holy and wholesome thought to pray for the dead (cf. 2 Mac. 12: 43–44).

The Sadducees did not accept belief in the resurrection of the body (see above, p. 25). It is hard to say what the common people believed, but the Pharisees were probably able to inculcate faith in resurrection of the dead through the prayers of the synagogue liturgy (see above, p. 51). In the parable of Dives and Lazarus, Jesus seems able to assume a popular belief in places of punishment and places of reward (cf. Lk 16:19–31). But probably many of the people were as unresponsive and unreceptive to the teaching of the Pharisees as to that of Christ. They could find texts in the Scriptures to support the view common in all times and places that the end of man and of beast is the same—for example Job 20: 7: 'Though his height mount up to the heavens, and his head reach to the clouds, he will perish for ever like his own dung,' and Ecclesiastes 3: 19: 'The fate of the sons of men and the fate of beasts is the same; as one dies, so dies the

56

other. They all have the same breath, and man has no advantage over the beasts; for all is vanity.'

About Forgiveness of Sin

It was believed that God had mercifully provided, in the sacrifices of the temple, the means whereby sins might be forgiven. The sinner must repent (and show his repentance in prayer, fasting and almsgiving); then the sacrifices, especially that of the Day of Atonement, would expiate his sins. According to the Mishnah (tractate Shebuoth, I, 6—Danby, p. 410),

> for uncleanness that befalls the Temple and its Hallowed Things through wantonness, atonement is made by the goat whose blood is sprinkled within the Holy of Holies and by the Day of Atonement; for all other transgressions spoken of in the Law, venial or grave, wanton or un-witting, conscious or unconscious, sins of omission or of commission, sins punishable by Extirpation or by death at the hands of the court, the scapegoat makes atonement.

It was also believed that a sinner's own death, willingly accepted, could expiate his sin. According to the Mishnah (tr. Sanhedrin, VI, 2—Danby, p. 390), before a condemned man was stoned, they said to him: 'Make thy confession', and if he said: 'May my death be an atonement for all my sins', he was sure of a share in the world to come. St Paul alludes to this belief in Romans 6: 7. It is not clear whether the death of a just man was believed to make expiation for the sins of others. The true meaning of Isaiah 53 was concealed in the Targum of the passage—as can be seen in William Manson, *Jesus the Messiah*, London, 1943, pp. 168–171, where translations of the text and of the Targum are printed in parallel columns. Manson observes that 'the Targum diverts the element of humiliation, suffering, and

C

death from the person of the Servant-Messiah and transfers it to Israel or to the heathen nations'.

Text	*Targum*
52: 13 Behold my Servant shall deal wisely, he shall be exalted. . . .	52: 13 Behold my Servant Messiah shall prosper, he shall be high. . . .
53: 4 Surely he hath borne our griefs, and carried our sorrows: yet we did esteem him stricken, smitten of God, and afflicted.	53: 4 Therefore for our sins he will pray, and our iniquities will for his sake be forgiven, although we were accounted stricken, smitten before the Lord, and afflicted.
5 But he was wounded for our transgressions, he was bruised for our iniquities; the chastisement of our peace was upon him; and with his stripes we are healed.	5 But he will build up the Holy Place, which has been polluted for our sins and delivered to the enemy for our iniquities; and by his instruction peace shall be increased upon us, and by devotion to his words our sins will be forgiven us.
6 All we like sheep have gone astray . . . and the Lord hath laid on him the iniquity of us all.	6 All we like sheep had been scattered . . . but it was the Lord's good pleasure to forgive these sins of all of us for his sake.
7 He was oppressed, yet he humbled himself, and opened not his mouth; as a lamb that is led to the slaughter . . . he opened not his mouth.	7 He prayed, and he was answered, and ere even he had opened his mouth, he was accepted: the mighty of the peoples he will deliver up like sheep to the slaughter.

About the History of Israel

The great miracles of Old Testament history, such as the drowning of Pharaoh's army in the Red Sea and the collapse of the walls of Jericho, were taken quite literally. Israel's political calamities were believed to be solely the result of disobedience to the Law. It was believed that if Israel would observe the Law, God would intervene again as in the Exodus from Egypt and the conquest of Canaan. Hence the repeated attempts of the Jews to throw off the Roman yoke.

Test

APOCALYPTIC LITERATURE

The term 'apocalyptic literature' is used to describe a number of Jewish books which conform, more or less, to a pattern set by the Book of Daniel, which was composed about 166 B.C. Some characteristics of this genre are:

1. It is deliberately pseudonymous. Prophecies referring to the present and future are put into the mouth of some worthy of the past. Examples are: The Book of Enoch, The Testaments of the Twelve Patriarchs, The Psalms of Solomon, The Assumption of Moses—and the Book of Daniel itself.

2. Past history is divided into periods, which mount towards a crisis. The crisis belongs to the writer's own time.

3. There are promises of a glorious change in the fortunes of Israel in the not too distant future—the 'world to come' or 'future aeon' is announced as being at hand.

4. These books are literary productions, not oral compositions like the works of the great Old Testament prophets. They make extensive use of bizarre imagery.

Writing during the Maccabean wars, the author of Daniel first tells a series of short stories (chapters 1–6) to which he gives a setting back in the time of Nebuchadnezzar; each story points a moral highly appropriate to the time of king Antiochus Epiphanes, the new Nebuchadnezzar. Then in chapters 7–12 he describes Daniel as seeing a series of prophetic visions which cover the period from Nebuchadnezzar to the Maccabean wars and a little beyond. They are explained to him by angels: shortly after the present crisis will come the Kingdom of God, in which Israel, 'the people of the saints of the Most High', represented by 'one like a son of man', will receive dominion from God.[1]

[1] On the Son of Man as a Second Adam, see E. W. Heaton, *The Book of Daniel*, London, 1956, pp. 169–190.

Jesus expressed his teaching within the apocalyptic framework. The evangelists sum up his proclamation in the formula 'Repent, for the kingdom of heaven is at hand' (Mk 1: 15)—the very idea of 'the kingdom of heaven' is from the apocalyptists. At the end of his public ministry, he spoke the Apocalyptic Discourse, in which he describes the signs of the End in phrases borrowed from Daniel—for example, 'abomination of desolation' is from Daniel 12: 11 (cf. Mk 13: 14). And when on trial before Caiaphas, he identified himself as 'the Son of Man.'

The *Wisdom of Solomon* (probably composed at Alexandria about 50 B.C., and almost certainly known to St Paul) has several of the features of apocalyptic literature.[1]

---

[1] Cf. J. P. M. Sweet, 'The Theory of Miracles in the Wisdom of Solomon', in C. F. D. Moule, *Miracles*, London, 1965, pp. 117–120.

MESSIANIC EXPECTATIONS

The Jews regarded the God of Israel as the Lord of history. They made no distinction between religious history and secular history, but learned their history and their religion from the same books. The whole of their history converged upon one conclusion: that the political situation in which they found themselves at the beginning of the first century was not what it ought to be and could not be permanent. As God's chosen people, they were not destined to remain for ever subject to the rule of idolatrous foreigners. One day, God would send his Messiah, a son of David, who would drive out the Roman imperialists and restore the kingdom to Israel, as in the days of David and Solomon. The apocalyptic literature fanned these hopes, and promised that the restoration would come soon.

The Messianic hope was not confined to any one sect. It took different forms among different parts of the population. At Qumran two Messiahs were expected, a King and a Priest. Many others expected a warrior Messiah who would establish a nationalistic kingdom, in which the Gentiles would serve the Jews. The pious poor may have had a more spiritual hope—see the *Magnificat* and *Benedictus*. Some Jews looked forward to a glorious future without giving much attention to the person of the Messiah.[1]

[1] On the history of the title 'Messiah' see pp. 116–7.

Some of the Jews did not feel obliged to wait patiently for the Messiah to come. They saw how the Maccabeans, fired with zeal for God's Law, had defeated the superior forces of Syria; and they believed that if they too took the initiative against Rome, God would come to their aid. Josephus calls them the 'Zealots'.

The Zealot movement began in A.D. 6, when Judas the Galilean and Sadduk a Pharisee led a revolt against the census of Quirinius. Josephus (*Ant.*, XVIII, 1, 9) regards these two men as the founders of a fourth sect (in addition to the Pharisees, Sadducees and Essenes), but Gamaliel says in Acts 5: 37 that the followers of Judas were scattered.

One of the disciples of Jesus was called Simon the Zealot. (Lk. 6:15; Acts 1:13).

In Tacitus's *Agricola*, the Scottish freedom-fighter Calgacus denounces the Romans thus (§ 30): 'Plunderers of the world! Now that there is no more land to satisfy their passion for universal devastation, they are combing the sea. If their enemy is rich, they lust for wealth; if he is poor, then for power—neither East nor West has sated their appetite—alone of all men they look with the same hungry eyes on wealth and poverty. Looting, slaughter, and rapine they cloak with the name of "empire", and where they make a wilderness they call it "peace".' Many in Palestine shared these sentiments; there was never real peace in Israel under the Romans.

In A.D. 6, the revolt of Judas the Galilean was put down with brutality: Quintilius Varus, the legate of Syria, crucified 2,000 rebels and took many slaves. The census was carried through, the procurators were installed, and tribute was levied. The fortress Antonia was garrisoned by Roman soldiers. The high-priestly vestments were kept under Roman control. The Sanhedrin was deprived of capital jurisdiction. These grievances and the harshness of Roman rule caused constant unrest.

In 30, there may have been a Messianic disturbance shortly before the arrest of Jesus. Mark 15: 7 says that 'Barabbas was in bonds along with the rioters who had caused bloodshed in the riot'.

In 36, Pilate suppressed a revolt in Samaria with so much bloodshed that he was deposed by the legate of Syria. In 39, the emperor Gaius caused a crisis by ordering that his statue be set up in the temple (see above, p. 16). In 44 occurred the revolt of Theudas mentioned (anachronistically?) in the speech of Gamaliel (Acts 5: 36). About 55, under the procurator Felix, occurred the revolt of the Egyptian Jew mentioned in Acts 21: 38.

In 66, the last procurator, Gessius Florus, confiscated seventeen talents from the temple treasury. This proved to be the last straw. As Tacitus says, 'the patience of the Jews lasted till Gessius Florus; then war broke out' (*Hist.*, V, 10).

In the apocalyptic literature, the establishment of the Messianic kingdom is always preceded by a period of suffering and oppression. The Zealots, therefore, saw in the maladministration of the procurators a sign that the kingdom was at hand. Josephus adds: 'But what more than all else excited them to the war was an ambiguous prophecy that at that time one from their country would become ruler of the world.' The reference may be to Daniel 7.

The revolt of 66 can hardly be called Messianic. It was not led by a Messianic pretender (as was the revolt of 132). A certain Manahem did claim to be king of Israel, but he was soon murdered.

At the beginning of the revolt, the Jews were encouraged by a victory over Cestius Gallus, the governor of Syria. Then Nero appointed Vespasian, who marched down with the Syrian legions. He mopped up Galilee and captured Josephus (see above, p. 1), then subdued Peraea, and arrived near Jerusalem. At this stage Nero died, and there was a lull in the war. For three years Jerusalem remained unmolested.

When Vespasian became emperor in 69, he entrusted the war to his son Titus, who besieged Jerusalem in 70. After four months of bitter fighting the temple was captured. The horrors of starvation within the city are graphically described by Josephus (*Wars*, V, quoted in Williamson's *Eusebius*, pp. 112–17). The temple was destroyed. Titus held a triumph at Rome, in which the seven-branch lampstand was carried as booty—as can be seen to this day in the bas relief of the Arch of Titus.

The fortress of Masada, on the west of the Dead Sea, held out nearly two years longer. In order to capture it, the Roman engineers built a huge causeway from the nearest mountain to the top of Masada. Corroded by the weather, it remains there to this day, to excite the wonder of tourists. When the Romans finally gained the summit, only one old woman remained alive. The rest of the defenders had killed themselves in pairs.

The war destroyed the temple and with it the Sadducees. It also destroyed Qumran and with it the Essenes. Pharisaism was preserved at Jamnia, whither Johannan ben Zakkai had escaped by having himself carried out of Jerusalem as one dead (see above, p. 2).

At the beginning of the war, the Christian community of Jerusalem fled to Pella, a city of the Decapolis. Jesus had warned them to flee when the crisis came (cf. Mk 13: 14). From this time, Jerusalem ceased to be the visible centre of the Church.[1]

[1] Cf. L. Goppelt, *Jesus, Paul and Judaism*, New York, 1964, p. 131.

Even the calamity of A.D. 70 could be regarded as a part of the eschatological tribulation. The Jews continued to hope.

In 114 Trajan attacked the Parthians, the only oriental power which Rome could not subdue. When it was rumoured that the campaign was not going well, the Jews of Alexandria, Cyrenaica and Cyprus rose in rebellion. Again they were crushed (115–17).

About 130, Hadrian ordered that a new city, to be called Aelia Capitolina, be built on the ruins of Jerusalem. It was to have a temple dedicated to Jupiter Capitolinus in which emperor-worship would be practised. This decision, implying that the Jewish temple would not be rebuilt, provoked the final revolt under a Jew named Simon. One of the leading rabbis, by name R. Akiba, declared that Simon was the Messiah and gave him the title Bar-Cochba ('Son of a Star'), a title derived from the prophecy of Balaam in Numbers 24: 17: 'A star shall come forth out of Jacob, and a sceptre shall rise out of Israel; it shall crush the forehead of Moab, and break down all the sons of Sheth.' (Letters of Bar-Cochba from the time of the war have been discovered south of Qumran.) According to Justin Martyr, Bar-Cochba inflicted terrible punishments on Christian Jews who would not blaspheme Jesus Christ and recognize himself as the Messiah.

The war lasted three years (132–35). Casualties on both sides were very heavy—about 850,000 in all. In the end, of course the Roman legions prevailed.

After the war, Aelia Capitolina was built as a Roman 'colony', and a temple of Jupiter Capitolinus was built, containing an equestrian statue of Hadrian. Jews were forbidden to enter the city; circumcision and observance of the sabbath were forbidden under pain of death. R. Akiba defied the edict and was put to death under great tortures. He died reciting the *Shema*, prolonging the last syllable: 'Hear, O Israel, the Lord thy God is one (*eha-a-ad*).' Before the war, he had been one of the two leading teachers. He was not discredited by the failure of the revolt. According to a Jewish legend, the subtlety of his exegesis astonished Moses himself, who had not perceived all the implications of what he wrote until R. Akiba pointed them out.

Test

What book set the pattern of apocalyptic literature?................................1

When was this book written?...2

Who were the founders of the Zealot movement, according
   to Josephus?..3

In what year did they revolt?...4

Who was the Roman general who suppressed their revolt?................5

In what year did Gaius order his statue to be set up in Jerusalem?.....6

Who was the legate of Syria who declined to obey? (16)...................7

Which speaker in Acts mentions the revolt of Theudas?...................8

The Roman officer in Acts 21 mentions the revolt of whom? 9

Who was the last procurator of Judaea?..10

In what year did he provoke the Jews to rebellion?.........................11

In what year was Jerusalem destroyed?...12

Who said: 'They make a desolation and call it peace'?....................13

Who was the leader of the resistance in Galilee? (1)........................14

What was the name of the last Jewish fortress to fall?.....................15

Who was the rabbi who inspired the revolt of 132?..........................16

What name did he give to the Messianic pretender?.........................17

From which prophecy did he derive this name?................................18

What was the name of the Roman colony founded on the
   site of Jerusalem? 19

What was Rabbi Akiba's last word?..20

THE FLAVIAN EMPERORS

VESPASIAN (Titus Flavius Vespasianus), emperor 69–79, was the son of a tax-gatherer. He earned military decorations during Claudius's campaign in Britain in 44. In 66 he accompanied Nero to Greece, and disgraced himself by falling asleep during one of the emperor's recitals. However, later in 66 he was appointed to suppress the Jewish revolt (see above, p. 67).

When he became emperor, he reorganized the empire's finances, and raised the tribute to be paid by the provinces. He began the building of the Colosseum.

He appointed Agricola, the father-in-law of Tacitus, to command the army in Britain. Agricola conquered North Wales and advanced the frontier into Scotland. He was recalled in 84 by Domitian, who was jealous of his successes.

TITUS—Vespasian was succeeded by his elder son Titus, who had completed the suppression of the Jewish revolt. During his brief reign from 79–81, the eruption of Vesuvius destroyed Pompeii and Herculaneum, and a great fire swept Rome.

DOMITIAN—Titus was succeeded by his younger brother Domitian, who was emperor from 81–96. He ruled well until 88, when Saturninus, the governor of Upper Germany, proclaimed himself emperor. The revolt failed; but from this time on Domitian became more and more suspicious and tyrannical.

According to Irenaeus, the Apocalypse was written during this reign. Its purpose is to prepare the reader for persecution, which is believed to be imminent.

In 96 Domitian's wife plotted with the two praetorian prefects, and Domitian was assassinated.

THE EMPERORS FROM NERVA TO MARCUS AURELIUS

NERVA—As Domitian left no issue, the senate selected Nerva as a man fit to rule. He was of noble birth, a good speaker, a peace-loving and just man, who could be expected to rule constitutionally. In his sixteen months of power (96–98), he carried out a policy of social reform, spending large sums on poor relief and land allotments. He adopted Trajan to be his successor, and died a natural death.

TRAJAN had served in Spain, Syria and Upper Germany, and was respected as a successful and popular general. As emperor, he carried on major campaigns in Dacia and Parthia (see p. 69). At Rome he extended the poor relief, and built the splendid Forum of Trajan with 'Trajan's Column' covered by a spiral relief commemorating the Dacian campaign. It stands there still, surmounted by a statue of St Peter.

In 107, Ignatius, the third bishop of Antioch, was thrown to the beasts in Rome. Trajan appointed the younger Pliny to be governor of Bithynia, and wrote to him telling him not to heed anonymous letters in which men and women were accused of being Christians. '*Pessimi exempli, nec nostri saeculi,*' he said—'It is a bad precedent, and jars with the spirit of our age.'

After ruling from 98–117, Trajan died in Cilicia, on his way back from Parthia. Just before his death, he adopted Hadrian to succeed him.

HADRIAN (Publius Aelius Hadrianus) was accepted by the senate and reigned from 117–38. He made great journeys through the provinces to organize defence and administration. In 121 he visited Britain and ordered the building of 'Hadrian's Wall' to keep out the Scots. In 130 he visited

Palestine and ordered the building of Colonia Aelia Capitolina on the ruins of Jerusalem, thus provoking the Jewish revolt of 132–35.

A famous martyr of Hadrian's reign was the aged Polycarp, executed at Smyrna in 135. (Eusebius, however, places this martydom in the reign of Antoninus Pius.)

ANTONINUS PIUS, who had been adopted by Hadrian, ruled from 138–61. He consolidated the frontiers and governed well. During his reign two prominent heresiarchs taught in Rome—Valentinus and Marcion. Justin Martyr, a native of Samaria, replied on behalf of the true faith.

MARCUS AURELIUS, the Stoic philosopher-emperor, had been adopted by Antoninus. Though war was distasteful to him, he had to spend much of his reign conducting wars. He left a book of *Meditations*, in which there is much to admire—for example (VII, 59): 'Look within! Within is the fountain of good always ready to well forth if thou wilt always delve' (cf. Jn 4: 14).

During his reign, Tatian composed his *Diatessaron* about 175, and Irenaeus, bishop of Lyons, composed his work *Against Heresies*. Marcus died in 180.

Test

About A.D. 3, Paul was born at Tarsus in Cilicia. As his father was a Roman citizen, he too was a Roman citizen from birth (Acts 22: 28). He learned both Greek and Hebrew from childhood, and was brought up as a Pharisee. In Acts 22: 3, he says that he was educated in Jerusalem and studied the Law 'at the feet of Gamaliel'. Since he was entrusted with authority to persecute Christians (and perhaps followers of John the Baptist too—cf. Acts 9: 2), he was probably an ordained rabbi. He may have been in Jerusalem during Christ's ministry, but does not say whether he ever saw him (cf. 2 Cor. 5: 16).

About 33–34, he was present at the stoning of Stephen (Acts 7: 58), an act contrary to Roman Law (see above, p. 20). After his conversion on the road to Damascus, he preached for a while in Damascus. At this time he must have received some instruction about the Christian 'traditions' (cf. 1 Cor. 11: 23–25). From Damascus he went into Arabia (Nabataea—see p. 109 below), probably to preach (cf. Gal. 1:17). When he returned to Damascus, king Aretas of Arabia tried to seize him, but he was let down from the walls of Damascus in a basket and escaped (2 Cor. 11: 32).

About 37, he paid his first visit to Peter in Jerusalem (Gal. 1: 18); and at this time, to judge from Acts 22: 17, he had a vision in the temple telling him to go to the Gentiles. This may have been the occasion when he was rapt up to the third heaven (2 Cor. 12: 2). He went away to Syria and Cilicia and preached the gospel. From 37–44, his movements are unrecorded. These are often called 'the silent years'.

About 44, Barnabas brought Paul from Tarsus to Antioch. After a year or more, these two were sent out on the FIRST MISSIONARY JOURNEY (Acts 11: 26). Churches were founded at Antioch-in-Pisidia, at Iconium and Lystra in Lycaonia, and at Derbe in the Regnum Antiochi (these cities were in the south of the Roman province of Galatia—see the map on p. 108).

In 49, after the return of Paul and Barnabas, a dispute broke out at Antioch as to whether Gentile converts should be circumcised and made to follow the Jewish way of life St. Paul maintained that they should not. The question was settled at the COUNCIL OF JERUSALEM (Acts 15: Gal. 2: 1–10). Paul's view was vindicated: the Church was not to remain a sect within Judaism.

In 49 or 50, back at Antioch after the Council, Paul fell out with Barnabas and the two parted. Paul set out on his SECOND MISSIONARY JOURNEY, during which he crossed into Europe and founded churches at Philippi, Thessalonica and Corinth. At Athens he was unsuccessful. At Corinth he was brought before the proconsul Gallio, whose period of office is known from an inscription at Delphi to have been in the years 51–52 and/or 52–53. This is one of the surest points in the chronology of St Paul's life.[1]

In 53 or 54, Paul revisited Jerusalem, and returned to Antioch. The dispute between Paul and Peter described in Galatians 2: 11–21 probably occurred at this time. (Some scholars think it took place just before or just after the Council in 49.) Then Paul set out on his THIRD MISSIONARY JOURNEY, during which he spent three years at Ephesus (part of the time probably in prison). Acts does not mention any new churches founded on this journey. In 58, Paul revisited Greece and spent three months at Corinth.

In 58, Paul returned to Jerusalem with money which he had collected for the poor. He was almost lynched in the temple, but was rescued by the Roman soldiers. He was tried before the Sanhedrin (Acts 22). After a plot against his life, he was transferred to Caesarea, where he was kept in prison for two years. In 60, he appealed to Caesar and was sent to Rome.

[1] Cf. F. Jackson and K. Lake, *The Beginnings of Christianity*, Vol. London, 1933, pp. 460–64.

In 61, after a shipwreck off Malta, he arrived in Rome, where again he spent two years in custody. Whether he was at length tried, and if so with what result, is not known. If released, he may have gone to Spain (cf. Rom 15: 24), or he may have returned to Ephesus, Macedonia and Crete (if he wrote 1 Tim. and Tit. at this time).

In 67, according to a strong and reliable tradition, he was martyred in Rome.

Note: In the Acts of the Apostles, the Council of Jerusalem is placed after the first missionary journey. Some American scholars have argued that it really took place after the second. This view fills up the 'silent years'—but it creates other difficulties.

CHRONOLOGICAL DISTRIBUTION OF ST PAUL'S EPISTLES

Written during the Second Missionary Journey:
1 and 2 Thessalonians, from Corinth.

Written during the Third Missionary Journey:
1 Corinthians, from Ephesus;
Galatians, probably from Ephesus;
2 Corinthians, from Macedonia;
Romans, from Corinth.

Written during the First Roman Captivity:
Probably Philippians, Colossians and Philemon, and Ephesians. (Another view is that these were written during an earlier imprisonment *at Ephesus*, not recorded in Acts.)

Written during the Interval of Freedom:
1 Timothy and Titus, if from the hand of Paul himself, were written at this time.

Written during the Second Roman Captivity:
2 Timothy, if from the hand of Paul, is his last spiritual testament.

Note: Some scholars place Galatians between 2 Corinthians and Romans. Some place it at the end of the first missionary journey, just before the Council.

Not all of St Paul's letters have survived. 2 Peter 3:16 shows that ecclesiastical authorities felt some reserve about them—they were easily misinterpreted. Those which have survived were probably collected and published as a corpus about A.D. 90, after a period of comparative neglect.[1] St Luke probably wrote Acts about A.D. 85 (see below, p. 86). He does not appear to have had access to the whole Pauline corpus.

[1] See further C. L. Mitton, *The Formation of the Pauline Corpus of Letters*, London, 1955.

Test

The Apostolic Fathers

The Epistle of Clement (of Rome) to the Corinthians is contained in the Codex Alexandrinus. It was written about A.D. 96, to foster peace in the church of Corinth. (The second Epistle of Clement is usually rejected as unauthentic on stylistic grounds, but recent computer tests do not confirm this judgment of the scholars.)

The Seven Epistles of Ignatius (of Antioch) were written by Ignatius when he was on his way to martyrdom in Rome, about A.D. 107. The term 'Catholic Church' appears for the first time in his Letter to the church of Smyrna. He is a stout defender of the 'monarchic episcopate': in each church there is to be one bishop representing Christ.

The Epistle of Polycarp (of Smyrna) to the Philippians is probably conflated from two epistles written in 110 and 135. It is a covering letter, sent with a copy of the Epistles of Ignatius.

The Fragments of Papias (of Hierapolis)—About 130, Papias wrote five books of *Explanations of the Logia of the Lord*, from which Eusebius quotes a few sentences about the origins of the gospels of Matthew and Mark. These are hard to interpret, but valuable because they are our earliest extra-biblical evidence about the evangelists.

The 'Shepherd' of Hermas—According to the Muratorian Canon (see p. 93), Hermas was the brother of Pius I, bishop of Rome. Parts of the *Shepherd* may have been written in the time of Clement (*c.* 96); the final editing is probably from the time of Pius (*c.* 150).

The following works by unknown authors are often printed with the works of the Apostolic Fathers:

The Didache, a collection of moral and liturgical instructions for Gentile Christians, may be the very earliest extracanonical Christian book which has survived. Its date is disputed; A.D. 80–100 seems likely. Its place of origin is also uncertain; the region of Antioch in Syria is a likely guess. It begins with a description of the Two Ways (the way of life and the way of death), which acquired great popularity in later moral collections.

The Epistle of Barnabas is not likely to be the work of St Paul's companion Barnabas. The author regards the Old Testament as the work of the devil (cf. 9:4). It was probably written about A.D. 125. It contains a description of the Two Ways; whether this is dependent on the *Didache*, or vice versa, or both on a lost source, is a matter of dispute.

The Letter to Diognetus, written about A.D. 125, is an attractive apologia for Christianity.

Controversialists of the Second Century

The 'Greek Apologists'—Quadratus, Aristides, Ariston of Pella, and Justin Martyr (on whom see above, p. 46)—wrote books in defence of the Christian faith.

Among authors who deviated from orthodoxy were the following: Basilides (*c.* 135), Valentinus (*c.* 150), and Heracleon (*c.* 160)—three Gnostics; Montanus (*c.* 125), who spread unacceptable views about prophecy and inspiration, and Marcion (*c.* 140), who drew up his own canon of Scripture.

In 1946 a library of Gnostic writings was discovered near the former monastery of Chenoboskion, at Nag-Hammadi, thirty miles north of Luxor in Egypt. They are referred to as 'the Chenoboskion manuscripts' or 'the Nag-Hammadi manuscripts'. When published and examined, these will doubtless cast light on the varieties of Christian opinion in the second century, and perhaps earlier.[1]

---

[1] Cf. J. Doresse, *The Secret Books of the Egyptian Gnostics*, London, 1960.

Eusebius names several writers who replied to Basilides, Marcion and other heretics, and whose works have perished. Fragments remain of the writings of HEGESIPPUS, probably a Jew, who went to Rome in the time of Pope Anicetus I (c. 154–66) to learn the true faith, and published his *Memoirs* about 180.

Much the most important writer of the second century is IRENAEUS, who had been a disciple of Polycarp in his youth. He left Asia Minor and became first a presbyter and then bishop (in 177) of the church of Lyons in France during the principate of Marcus Aurelius. His main work, known as the *Adversus Haereses*, was called in the Greek original 'A Refutation and Rejection of the so-called Gnosis'. It is preserved in a Latin translation, which is complete, and in fragments of the Greek and portions of Armenian and Syriac translations.

THEOPHILUS, bishop of Antioch (c. 185), wrote a lost work against Marcion. His main work, *Ad Autolycum*, is an apologia addressed to educated pagans.

MELITO, bishop of Sardes in Lydia (c. 175), wrote against Montanus and Marcion, and addressed an Apology to Marcus Aurelius. In 1940 a Sermon on the Passion by Melito was published from a fourth-century papyrus.[1]

[1] For further information on these early Christian writings, see B. Altaner, *Patrology*, Edinburgh, 1960, or J. Quasten, *Patrology*, Utrecht, 1950, Vol. I (The Beginnings of Patristic Literature).

Test

Which ancient author preserved the fragments of Papias?...............1

What was the title of Papias's book?.................................2

To whom did Clement send his First Epistle?.........................3

When did he write it?...4

Name the brother of Hermas mentioned in the Muratorian
Canon 5

To which church is the Epistle of Polycarp addressed?..............6

Which of the Apostolic Fathers defends the monarchic
episcopate? 7

For whom was the *Didache* written?................................8

Name a non-Christian document in which there is a description of the Two Ways (37)..9

When was the Epistle of Barnabas written?.........................10

Where were Gnostic manuscripts found in 1946?.....................11

Of which church did Irenaeus become bishop, and when?.............12

What is the title of Irenaeus's main work?........................13

What is the title of Justin's main work? (46).....................14

Which of these early writers first uses the phrase 'Catholic
Church'? 15

Which early heretic spread false views about prophecy?............16

When did Barnabas summon Paul to Antioch? (76)....................17

Of which rabbi was Paul a pupil? (76).............................18

When does Irenaeus say the Apocalypse was written? (72)...........19

Under which emperor was Polycarp martyred? (74)...................20

84

THE DATING OF MATTHEW–MARK–LUKE–ACTS

According to Irenaeus (*c.* 180), St Mark wrote his gospel after the deaths of Peter and Paul. But Clement of Alexandria (*c.* 225) says that St Mark's gospel was shown to Peter, who neither encouraged nor forbade its diffusion. Most scholars date the composition of Mark shortly before or after the death of St Peter, i.e. between 64 and 70.

Luke is certainly dependent on Mark, and the great majority of scholars think that Matthew is too. As Luke 19: 43 to 44 seems to show knowledge of the encirclement and destruction of Jerusalem in A.D. 70, the third gospel should probably be dated about 75. A similar argument from Matthew 22: 7 leads to the conclusion that the first gospel was written about this time too.[1] Neither Matthew nor Luke (in his gospel) shows any acquaintance with the Pauline Epistles.

It seems, then, that Mark is to be dated about 65, and Matthew and Luke about 75. But many scholars think that these three canonical gospels are fairly late representatives of a tradition of gospel writing (Luke 1: 1 knows of 'many' who have previously put their hand to this task); all three—and perhaps the fourth gospel too—go back to a Greek translation of the Hebrew or Aramaic compilation mentioned by Papias: 'Matthew drew up the Logia in the Hebrew language, and each one translated them as best he could.' Recent developments in the structural analysis of the gospels point to the conclusion that this gospel was made in the church of Jerusalem before the circumcision controversy blew up in A.D. 49. Several of the gospel stories show signs of having been used by both sides in this controversy—e.g. the cure of the Syrophoenician woman's daughter (compare Matthew 15: 21–28 with Mark 7: 24–30).

[1] C. A. Wikenhauser, *New Testament Introduction*, Edinburgh, 1958, pp. 198 and 221.

The narrative of Acts breaks off in A.D. 62. Some scholars have inferred that St Luke wrote Acts in 62 in Rome. But it is difficult to believe that while in close contact with Paul, Luke could have written an account of the circumcision crisis so different from that given by Paul in the Epistle to the Galatians. Moreover, few scholars are willing to hold that St Luke wrote Acts before his gospel (which is dependent on Mark). If he wrote his gospel about 75, he may have completed Acts about 80–85. This date suits the main purpose of Acts, which is to explain to second generation Gentile Christians where their religion came from.

Which ancient author says that Mark was shown to Peter?............1

Which ancient author says that Peter died before Mark was written? 2

When was St Peter put to death?..3

What date do most scholars assign to Mark? 4

What is a probable date for the composition of Luke? 5

Did St Luke write Acts before or after his gospel?......................6

In what year does the narrative of Acts break off?......................7

What was the outcome of St Paul's trial before Caesar?.............8

What is a probable date for the composition of Acts?.................9

Who said 'Matthew drew up the Logia in the Hebrew language'? 10

What is a probable date for the composition of this 'Aramaic Matthew'? 11

Which parable in Matthew seems to show knowledge of the destruction of Jerusalem?..12

In what year was Jerusalem destroyed? (67)............................13

What is a probable date for the composition of the canonical Greek Matthew? 14

Who was the emperor when Jerusalem was destroyed? (72)....15

Was the Syrophoenician woman a Jewess or a Gentile?..........16

In which gospel does Christ say to her: 'I am sent only to the lost sheep of the house of Israel'?.......................................17

In which gospel does he say to her: 'First let the children be satisfied; it is not right to take the children's bread and throw it to dogs'?...18

THE EARLY HISTORY OF THE FOURTH GOSPEL

Ignatius of Antioch—The Letters of Ignatius contain three possible allusions to the fourth gospel—which is very little. The silence of Ignatius with regard to St John's gospel is an enigma.

Papias—Eusebius quotes Papias's comments on the origin of Matthew and Mark, but not on Luke or John. Probably the only gospels known to Papias were Matthew and Mark.

Polycarp—According to Irenaeus, Polycarp was a disciple of St John. Yet Polycarp's Letter to the Philippians reveals no knowledge of St John's gospel. Matthew is Polycarp's gospel.

It is therefore very difficult to believe that the fourth gospel was published at Ephesus in the nineties of the first century as the work of St John the Apostle.

From Tertullian (*De praescriptione haereticorum*, 38), we learn that Valentinus (see above, p. 82), author of *The Gospel of Truth*, used all four gospels. The first commentary on St John was written at Rome by a disciple of Valentinus named Heracleon about A.D. 160.

Justin—The first orthodox writer to commend the fourth gospel and the Logos doctrine to the church of Rome was Justin Martyr, and even he does not make bold use of it.

Melito—In his Homily on the Passion, written about 160 to 170, Melito is clearly dependent on the fourth gospel.

Theophilus of Antioch—In his *Ad Autolycum*, written about 180, Theophilus is the first author to quote the fourth gospel and attribute it to 'John'. But he does not say that 'John' was an apostle.

Irenaeus is the first author who unequivocally attributes the fourth gospel to John the Apostle: 'Then John the disciple of the Lord, the one who reclined on his breast, published his gospel, while he was living at Ephesus in Asia.' The later Fathers all follow Irenaeus, but modern scholars have misgivings about his testimony, on account of the silence of Ignatius and Polycarp and the slowness of this gospel to gain acceptance among Catholics.

The earliest known fragments of any New Testament manuscript is a papyrus belonging to the Rylands collection, acquired by the famous papyrologist A. S. Hunt in 1920 and published by C. H. Roberts in 1935. It contains John 18: 31–33; 37–38. The fourth gospel was, therefore, circulating in Egypt during the first half of the second century, probably before 135.

Test

Who is the first author who says that St John published his gospel at Ephesus?...1

Was the fourth gospel known to Papias?...2

Do Ignatius and Polycarp make much use of Matthew?...................3

Do they make much use of the fourth gospel?...................................4

Who is the first author who is known to have used all four gospels?..5

Who was the author of the first commentary on St John's gospel?...6

Which Roman writer first made tentative use of John...................7

What is the probable date of the Rylands papyrus of John 18?.....8

How many Epistles of Ignatius are extant? (81)...............................9

Of what see was Papias bishop? (81)...10

Of what see was Polycarp bishop? (81)..11

Of what see was Melito bishop? (83)...12

Which work of Melito's shows knowledge of John........................13

When did Tatian compose his *Diatessaron*? (74).........................14

Of what group were the Pharisees an offshoot (28)......................15

Name the Gnostic heresiarch who came from Samaria (46).....16

What is the Greek translation of the Bible called? (47)..............17

What does the word 'Diaspora' mean? (47)....................................18

What did the Jews call the abode of the dead? (54)......................19

To what family did Mariamne belong? (8).......................................20

90

At Antioch at the end of the first century, probably Matthew was the only gospel in use. Ignatius has a couple of possible allusions to Luke and three possible allusions to John, but is quite clearly dependent on Matthew.

At Rome, Clement used Matthew, Mark and Luke when composing his First Epistle. The heretic Valentinus used all four about 125. Among Catholics, the fourth gospel gained acceptance between 150 and 170. By about 170 the four gospels are so firmly established as a group that Tatian, author of the famous gospel-harmony, called it the *Diatessaron* (Greek for 'through four').

The first author who mentions all four gospels by name and explicitly treats them as a group is Irenaeus. He tries to prove, by theological reasons, that there must be four gospels and not less than four gospels:

> Since there are four corners of the earth and four principal winds (*pneumata*), and the Church is sown over the whole earth, and the gospel is the pillar and support of the Church and the breath (*pneuma*) of life, it is fitting that the Church should have four columns which blow incorruptibility in all directions and stir up the fires of human life. Hence it is clear that the Lord, the Architect of the universe, who is throned on the cherubim and holds all things together, after appearing to mankind, should give us the gospel in fourfold form (*tetramorphon*), but held together by one Spirit.

In other words, the gospels are the air-conditioning system built into the structure of the Church by the divine Architect —a remarkable anticipation of K. Rahner's views on inspiration.[1]

[1] Cf. K. Rahner, *Inspiration and the Bible*, Edinburgh, 1961.

However, it was probably a common feeling that the acceptance of four gospels which present so many problems of harmonization was an embarrassment. The heretic Marcion accepted only Luke, which he abbreviated. Tatian compiled his *Diatessaron*, to combine all four. In Syria, about 150, an apocryphal Gospel of Peter was written—an attempt to replace the four by one authoritative gospel under the name of the prince of the apostles.[1]

---

[1] Cf. O. Cullmann, 'The Plurality of the Gospels as a Theological Problem in Antiquity', in his collection of essays, *The Early Church*, London, 1956, pp. 39–58.

THE EARLY HISTORY OF THE NEW TESTAMENT CANON

The 'Canon' is a list of books which are approved for public reading in the liturgy and are a 'rule' by which to judge sound doctrine. (The Greek *kanon* means 'rule' or 'ruler'.) The word does not appear to have been used in this ecclesiastical sense before about A.D. 250.

The earliest extant canon of the New Testament Scriptures is the MURATORIAN CANON, part of a manuscript written in the seventh or eighth century, discovered in the Ambrosian Library at Milan by an Italian historian named Muratori and published by him in 1740. Lagrange refused to accept it as an official canon of the Roman Church, because it omits Hebrews, James and 1–2 Peter, and it includes the Apocalypse of Peter. However, there were minor uncertainties in all the other churches of the third and fourth centuries, and complete agreement was not reached until the time of Athanasius (who established the canonicity of Hebrews in the East) and Augustine (who established the canonicity of the Apocalypse in the West).

The state of the canon at the beginning of the second century can be inferred from the use made of the New Testament books by Clement (*c.* 95), Ignatius (*c.* 105), and Polycarp (*c.* 135). In this period we see the New Testament writings steadily advancing towards the status previously accorded to the Old Testament Scriptures (e.g. in the Pauline Epistles). In Clement, Old Testament quotations predominate; in Ignatius, New Testament allusions are as frequent as Old Testament quotations; in Polycarp, the New Testament predominates. Marcion carried this process to excess by rejecting the Old Testament altogether.

Marcion was a wealthy shipowner from Sinope in Pontus. He came to Rome, and by 144 was excommunicated. He maintained that the God of the Old Testament is not identical with the God of the New Testament. The God of the Old Testament is the Creator-God and the avenging God of justice; the God of the New Testament, on the other hand, is the Father of Mercy and the God of all consolation. He held that the original apostles had immediately contaminated Christ's teaching with an admixture of Jewish doctrine; Paul was the only genuine preacher of Christ. In accordance with these views,

(1) he dethroned the Old Testament Scriptures;
(2) he formed a new body of Scripture: a shortened gospel of St Luke (without the Infancy Narratives), and the Pauline Epistles (without the Pastorals);
(3) he put this collection in the place of the Old Testament Scriptures.

He left it to his disciples to complete the work of expurgation which he had begun.

The earliest official canons of the Church were probably issued in reply to Marcion, though the earliest decisions as to what could and what could not be read in the liturgy must have been made much before this time. In A.D. 220, Tertullian implies (*De Pudicitia*, 11) that several Councils had issued canons.

Test

According to Acts (2: 42; 4: 4), the Christian community in Jerusalem quickly grew to 3,000 and 5,000 members. In the early days, the disciples met in the temple in Solomon's Colonnade, and 'broke bread' in private houses (Acts 2: 46). It is not recorded whether Christian synagogues were ever opened in Jerusalem.

In the very early years (30–34), there were attempts by Annas and Caiaphas to silence and suppress the movement (cf. Acts 4). Stephen was executed for speaking against the Law (c. 33), and Paul persecuted Christians out of zeal for the Law (cf. Gal. 1: 14; Phil. 3: 6). When Paul was converted, the persecution subsided. After this, the Christians of Jerusalem were careful to observe the Law; so long as they did so, they were tolerated by the authorities. The Sadducees, and particularly the house of Annas, retained a latent hostility, but the Pharisees appear to have taken the tolerant attitude expressed by Gamaliel in his speech in Acts 5: 35–9.

The three 'pillars' of the Church were at first Peter and the two sons of Zebedee, James and John. In 44, when Herod Agrippa I put this James to the sword (Acts 12: 2), his place was taken by James 'the brother of the Lord', who became head of the church of Jerusalem until his execution in 62. Just after the execution of James the son of Zebedee, St Peter was imprisoned and miraculously rescued (Acts 12). After this he appears to have travelled in other parts of Judaea. (The position of James at this time was comparable to that of Linus and Anacletus in St Peter's last years at Rome.)

There is no reliable record of the activities of the other nine apostles. Presumably they did not work in the Greek-speaking world, for none of the Apostolic Fathers claims to be a disciple of any of them. The Philip mentioned by Papias as having lived at Hierapolis in Phrygia with his daughters was probably Philip the Deacon (Eusebius, III, 39).

In A.D. 49, Paul and Barnabas met James the brother of the Lord, Peter and John in Jerusalem for the Apostolic Council, at which it was agreed that Gentile converts should not be required to judaize.

In 58, when St Paul returned to Jerusalem for the last time, James warned him that the 'many thousands' of believers in Judaea had been told that he was teaching the Jews of the Diaspora to abandon the Law (Acts 21: 21). At James's suggestion, Paul gave a public demonstration of his fidelity to the Law (21: 26); but even so, he was almost lynched. He was rescued by Roman soldiers, and tried before the Sanhedrin.

In 62 James the brother of the Lord was executed. Eusebius (III, 23) quotes a long account by Hegesippus, who says that James was making too many converts among the ruling class. James was succeeded as bishop of Jerusalem by Symeon, 'a cousin of the Lord', who was martyred in the time of Trajan.

At the beginning of the war in 66, the Christian community migrated to Pella in the Decapolis, in obedience to a revelation (Eusebius, III, 5, 3). After this, Jerusalem ceased to be regarded as the centre of the Church.

Unfortunately, there is no record of the early history of the church of Alexandria. From the story of Apollos in Acts 18: 24–25 it appears that the doctrine and baptism of John the Baptist had reached Alexandria before 55, but not the gospel of Christ. Apollos first learned the gospel from St Paul's friends Aquila and Priscilla at Ephesus. After this, he preached successfully at Corinth. It is a reasonable guess that he also went back and preached in Alexandria.

Eusebius (II, 16, 1) records a tradition that St Mark was the first to preach at Alexandria. There is nothing unlikely in this. St Mark did not abandon the life of a missionary when he turned back from Perge in Pamphilia during St Paul's first missionary journey (Acts 13: 13). According to 1 Peter 5: 13 he was in Rome with St Peter; and in Colossians 4: 10 St Paul recommends him to the hospitality of the Colossians.

Ephesus was the administrative centre of the Roman province of Asia. St Paul made it his headquarters during his third missionary journey, and spent three years there. It is questionable whether he was the first to preach in the city. Aquila and Priscilla settled there before he did (cf. Acts 18: 19). When St Paul came to stay, he found some disciples of John the Baptist there (Acts 19: 1–7), and may have found some Christians too.

For about two years he gave daily lectures or instructions 'in the school of Tyrannus' (19: 9). Presumably he had the use of a lecture-hall when the professors of rhetoric or philosophy were not using it. St Luke's narrative of Paul's Ephesian ministry is disappointingly jejune. He reports the amusing incident of the confounding of the sons of Scaeva and the riot of the silversmiths; but he gives us not a glimpse of the community life of the Ephesian church.

On his last journey to Jerusalem, St Paul summoned the 'presbyters' of Ephesus to Miletus and exhorted them to care for the flock over which the Holy Spirit had appointed them 'bishops' (20: 28). There is no suggestion here of the monarchic episcopate. Some scholars have inferred from 1 Timothy 1: 3 that Timothy was the first monarchic bishop of Ephesus; but he appears to have been fulfilling only a temporary charge there (cf. 2 Tim. 4: 9).

Later, St John took up residence at Ephesus. Irenaeus (*Adv. Haer.*, III, 4, 3) records that on one occasion 'John, the disciple of the Lord, going to bathe at Ephesus, and perceiving Cerinthus within, rushed out of the bath-house without bathing, exclaiming, "Let us fly, lest even the bath-house fall down, because Cerinthus, the enemy of truth, is within".' In the Apocalypse, the first of the Letters to the Seven Churches is addressed to Ephesus; the Ephesians are charged with having allowed their first love to grow cold

(2: 4). After his release from Patmos, John must have returned to Ephesus, since, according to Papias, he was buried there (Eusebius, V, 24, 3).

Irenaeus says that St John published his gospel while living at Ephesus; but it seems doubtful whether this can be true. See above, p. 89.

Antioch on the Orontes was the administrative centre of the Roman province of Syria. It was the third largest city of the empire, Rome being the first and Alexandria the second. (St Paul was not the first to preach the gospel in any of these cities.)

The church at Antioch was founded by fugitives from the persecution at the time of Stephen's martyrdom (Acts 11). From the beginning it included Gentile as well as Jewish members. When the apostles heard of this foundation, they sent Barnabas to Antioch. He summoned Paul from Tarsus.

The first Gentile missions were sent out, not from Jerusalem (as we might have expected), but from Antioch (cf. Acts 13: 1–3): Barnabas and Paul went to Cyprus and Galatia, and returned to Antioch.

The Council of Jerusalem in 49 was occasioned by a deputation from Antioch (Acts 15). After the Council, Paul and Barnabas had a sharp disagreement over John Mark and decided to part company (Acts 16). Paul went off on his second journey with Silas, and eventually returned to Antioch. Probably it was on this occasion that he came into conflict with St Peter in the 'Antioch Incident' described in Galatians 2: 11–21 (but many scholars think the incident took place about the same time as the dispute with Barnabas, i.e. before the second journey). After his third journey St Paul did not return to Antioch.

Some modern writers think that the Gospel according to St Matthew was produced in the church of Antioch. The *Didache* too may come from this region.

At the close of the century, Antioch had as its bishop Ignatius, who was thrown to the beasts in the arena at Rome in about A.D. 107. He is a great protagonist of the monarchic

101

episcopate, which appears to have been established sooner at Antioch than elsewhere.

At Antioch the disciples were first called 'Christians', says St Luke (Acts 11). The only other writer of the first century who uses the word is Ignatius of Antioch. St Paul never uses it.

Corinth was the administrative centre of the Roman province of Achaea. St Paul arrived in 50 and stayed eighteen months. The foundation of the church of Corinth was the greatest achievement of his second missionary journey (Acts 18: 1–18).

After his departure, Apollos was recommended to the church of Corinth by Aquila and Priscilla, probably without St Paul's knowledge. His preaching was a great success (18: 27–28). Some members of the church of Corinth apparently preferred him to Paul. In his First (extant) Epistle to the Corinthians, St Paul shows some anxiety to maintain his own influence at Corinth. While warning the Corinthians that they must not set too much store by learning and rhetoric, he puts into the letter some splendid rhetoric of his own; and while disparaging the cult of personalities, he allows himself to point out, tactfully and in metaphors, that although he and Apollos are fellow workers, they are not to be held in equal esteem: Paul has planted, Apollos has watered; Paul 'like a skilful architect' has laid the founder tion, Apollos is one of several who have built upon it.

In the interval between the writing of the First and Second Epistles, some serious crisis occurred at Corinth. St Paul paid a brief visit, met with open insubordination, and went away (2 Cor. 2: 1). After his departure, he wrote a severe letter which has perished (unless it is preserved in 2 Cor. 10–13). Titus was entrusted with the unenviable task of delivering this letter, and was told to return through Macedonia and report to Paul at Troas. But Paul was anxious and went to meet him in Macedonia, where, to his intense relief, he was told that the Corinthians regretted their insubordination and had severely punished the ringleader of the opposition. St Paul expresses his relief at the beginning of 2 Corinthians. Later in the same year 57, he spent three months at Corinth.

We hear no more of the church of Corinth until the end of the century, when Clement of Rome sends another Epistle to the Corinthians. Again the spirit of insubordination is among them. Clement argues that the 'presbyters' or 'bishops' hold their authority from God and may not be deposed (cf. 42, 4 and 44, 5).

It is not known who first preached the gospel in Rome. Suetonius, in his *Life of Claudius* (25, 4), says that 'since the Jews were constantly rioting at the instigation of one Chrestus, Claudius expelled them from Rome'. This probably means that the introduction of Christianity split the large Jewish community of Rome and caused breaches of the peace. Aquila and Priscilla, who left Rome on account of this edict, may have been Christians before they met St Paul at Corinth in 50 (Acts 18: 2).

St Paul wrote his Epistle to the Romans in 58, at a time when he was hoping that after his last visit to Jerusalem he would be able to pass through Rome on his way to Spain. He writes to commend his mission and his gospel of Gentile freedom to the Christians of Rome, both Jews and Gentiles, and hints that he hopes they will help to finance his mission in Spain (cf. Rom. 15: 27–29). There is no suggestion in this Epistle that St Peter had already arrived in Rome.

When St Paul arrived in Rome in 61, although he was a prisoner, he was able to 'preach the kingdom of God and teach about the Lord Jesus Christ openly and unhindered' (Acts 28: 31).

It is nowhere explicitly stated in the New Testament that Peter went to Rome; but according to 1 Peter 5: 13, Peter and Mark are in 'Babylon'—which is doubtless a cryptic name for Rome. The tradition that Peter visited Rome and was martyred there is now generally accepted. The careful study by Oscar Cullmann, *Peter: Disciple, Apostle, Martyr*, has had great influence.

The first persecution was under Nero, after the fire of 64. But St Peter and St Paul were probably martyred a few years later, about 67. St Peter probably arrived in Rome after St Paul, in the early or middle 60s.

Vespasian and Titus did not continue the persecution. In the second half of the reign of Domitian, Clement mentions in his Epistle to the Corinthians 'sudden and repeated calamities' which have befallen the church of Rome. (This Epistle does not, like the Epistles of Ignatius a few years later, extol the monarchic episcopate as an instrument of peace and unity.)

The persecution of Christians was not pressed by Trajan. Ignatius of Antioch, on his way to martyrdom in Rome, was afraid that his friends might intervene and save him. In his Letter to Pliny, Trajan says that 'Christians are not to be sought out; but if they are accused and convicted, they must be punished.'

Test

In which part of the temple did the earliest Christians meet? 1

In what year was James the son of Zebedee executed? 2

In what year was James the brother of the Lord executed? 3

Who succeeded this James as bishop of Jerusalem? 4

Where did St Paul make his headquarters during the third
   journey? 5

Whom did he send to make peace between himself and the
   Corinthians? 6

From where and when did he write 2 Corinthians? 7

Where in the city of Ephesus did he give his lectures? 8

What is the cryptic name for Rome in 1 Peter? 9

What were the three largest cities in the Roman empire? 10

Where was Apollos born and educated? 11

By whom was he instructed in the gospel? 12

In which Epistle does St Paul speak about him? 13

In which city did St John encounter Cerinthus? 14

Where were the disciples first called 'Christians'? 15

In what year was St Paul arrested in Jerusalem? (77) 16

On which of his three journeys did he found the church of
   Corinth (77) 17

Where were Gnostic manuscripts found in 1946? (82) 18

Of which church did Irenaeus become bishop? (83) 19

In what year does the narrative of Acts break off? (86) 20

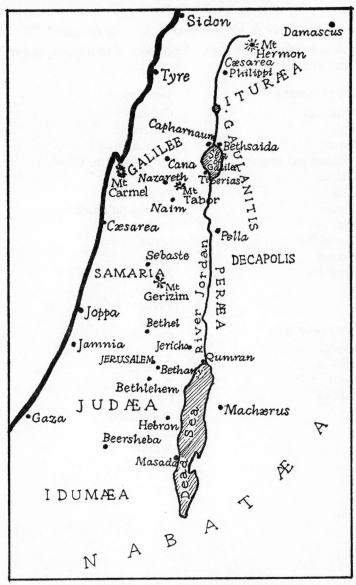

With this map before you, compare Matthew 3: 5–6 with Matthew 4: 24–25 and Mark 3: 7.

Could you mark in the following on the map opposite?
(Do not write on the page. Use a piece of thin typing paper. Then check with p. 108.)

The provinces of	*The cities of*
Cyrenaica	Cyrene
Egypt	Alexandria
Syria	Caesarea
Bithynia and Pontus	Antioch (on the Orontes)
Galatia	Tarsus
Asia	Perga
Thrace	Antioch (in Pisidia)
Dacia	Iconium
Macedonia	Lystra
Achaea	Derbe
Illyricum	Pessinus
	Ancyra
	Tavium
The islands of	Sinope
	Colossae
Cyprus	Hierapolis
Rhodes	Ephesus
Crete	Troas
Patmos	Philippi
	Thessalonica
	Beroea
	Athens
	Corinth

Could you mark in the following on the map opposite?

The sea of Galilee
The river Jordan
The Dead Sea
Bethsaida
Capharnaum
Tiberias
Pella
Sebaste
Jericho
Qumran
Machaerus
Masada
Gaza
Tyre
Sidon
Damascus
Caesarea Philippi
Caesarea
Joppa
Jamnia

Idumaea
Ituraea
Judaea
Samaria
Galilee
Gaulanitis
The Decapolis
Peraea
Arabia (Nabataea)
Jerusalem
Bethlehem
Bethany
Nazareth
Cana
Naim
Mt Tabor
Mt Hermon
Mt Gerizim
Mt Carmel

The regions ruled by
  Herod the Great
  Archelaus
  Herod Antipas
  Philip the Tetrarch
  Pontius Pilate
  Herod Agrippa I

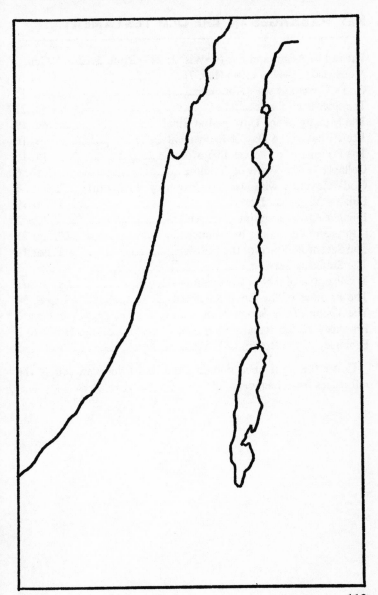

KEY PASSAGES IN THE OLD TESTAMENT

The fall of Adam and Eve (→Wis. 2: 24→Rom. 5:12)............Gen. 3
Melchisedek (→Ps. 110→Heb. 7) ....Gen. 14
God's Covenant with Abraham..................................Gen. 15
The Sacrifice of Isaac ....Gen. 22
The Making of the Covenant at Sinai..........................Exod. 19
The Ritual of the Day of Atonement...........................Lev. 16
The Promise of a Prophet like Moses..........................Deut. 18: 15
Collapse of the Walls of Jericho.............................Josh. 6
God's Covenant with David (=Prophecy of Nathan)..............2 Sam. 7
Elijah's Vision at Horeb ....1 Kgs 19
Elijah's Assumption into Heaven ....2 Kgs 2
Capture of Jerusalem by Nebuchadnezzar.......................2 Kgs 25
The Sevenfold Spirit of the Messiah..........................Isa. 11
The Suffering Servant..Isa. 53
The Promise of a New Covenant (→Heb 8).......................Jer. 31: 31
The Promise of the Good Shepherd ....Ezech. 34
The Vision of the Son of Man.................................Dan. 7
Prophecy of the Resurrection ....Hosea 6: 2
Prophecy of the Return of Elijah.............................Mal. 4: 5

Cover the right hand column, and see if you can supply the references from memory.

MILESTONES IN OLD TESTAMENT HISTORY

Call of Abraham ....1960 Genesis
   Exile in Egypt

Exodus from Egypt under Moses ⎫ Exodus
   Covenant at Sinai   1250 ⎬ Lev., Num.
                                   ⎭ Deut.

Entry into Canaan under Joshua 1200 Joshua
   Period of the Judges ⎱ Judges
Saul anointed King ....1020 ⎱ 1–2 Sam.
David anointed King...................1000 ⎰

Solomon anointed King ....961 ⎫
Building of First Temple ....950 ⎪
Death of Solomon, division of ⎪
   Kingdom ....922 ⎬ 1–2 Kgs ⎰ Amos
Fall of N. Kingdom to Assyrians....722 ⎪ { Hosea
Reform of Josiah ....620 ⎭ ⎱ I Isaiah

Capture of Jerusalem by ⎧ Habakkuk
   Nebuchadnezzar ....587 ⎪ Jeremiah
   Exile in Babylon ⎬ II Isaiah
                                 ⎩ Ezechiel
Return of Exiles under Zerubbabel 537 ⎫
Building of Second Temple......520–515 ⎪ Ezra and ⎧ Haggai and
Dedication of Walls of Jerusalem 444 ⎬ Nehemiah ⎨ Zechariah
Ministry of Ezra, Renewal of ⎪ ⎩ Malachi
   Covenant ....428 ⎭

Death of Alexander the Great,
   Origin of Successor Kingdoms 323
Judaea comes under the Ptolemies 301
Judaea comes under the Seleucids 197
Revolt of the Maccabees ....164 1–2 Macc., Daniel
Pompey captures Jerusalem 63

The word 'Messiah' means 'Anointed'. It did not acquire its technical meaning (the King who will fulfil the hopes of Israel) before the first century B.C.

The stream of Israelite hope, which runs through the centuries to the Messiah, begins from the promise made to Abraham (Gen. 15: 5): 'Look towards heaven and number the stars, if you are able to number them. . . . So shall your descendants be.' These words seemed to promise world-rulership (cf. Rom. 4: 13).

The hope of Israel was transformed into expectation of a 'Son of David' as a result of the prophecy of Nathan, who said to David (2 Sam. 7: 12–13): 'When your days are fulfilled and you lie down with your fathers, I will raise up your son after you . . . and I will establish the throne of his kingdom for ever.' As this divine promise was not fulfilled in Solomon and his successors, it was understood to be a promise for the remoter future.

King David is called the Lord's Anointed (Messiah) in Psalm 2: 2: 'The rulers take counsel together against the Lord and his Anointed.' But the major prophets, when they speak of the promised Son of David, do not call him 'the Messiah' (see Isa. 9: 1–2, 6–7; Jer. 32: 14–15; Ezek. 34: 11, 15–16, 22–24). II Isaiah actually calls Cyrus, the pagan king of Persia, God's 'Messiah' in Isaiah 45: 1.

After the Exile, the prophets Haggai and Zechariah announced to the little remnant at Jerusalem that their leader Zerubbabel was the promised Davidic ruler (cf. Zech. 6: 9–15). However, the title which they gave him was not 'Messiah' but 'Branch' (from Jer. 23: 5). Zerubbabel faded out, and the hope of a new Davidic kingdom almost died.

116

Hope was revived by the military successes of the Maccabees against Syria. In the Book of Daniel the traditional expectations are reformulated, without mention of a Son of David (probably because the Maccabees could not claim Davidic descent), in the vision of 'one like a son of man' (7: 14): 'and to him was given dominion and glory and kingdom, that all peoples, nations and languages should serve him.' The overthrow of the *beasts* (pagan empires) and the exaltation of *man* (the Israelite empire) to world-rulership is a restoration of the original order of creation (cf. Gen. 1: 28) which had been upset by sin.

'Messiah' appears as a title of the expected Son of David in the apocryphal *Similitudes of Enoch*, composed about 95–80 B.C., and in the Pharisaic *Psalms of Solomon*, composed about 50 B.C., alongside various other titles, such as 'the Elect One' and 'the Righteous One'. Of these *Psalms* no. 17 is the best known. It embodies a Messianic hope which is nationalistic and political, and yet at the same time spiritual and religious. Here is a part of it: 'Wisely, righteously he (the Son of David) shall thrust out sinners from the inheritance; he shall destroy the pride of the sinner as a potter's vessel. With a rod of iron he shall break in pieces all their substance; he shall destroy the godless nations with the word of his mouth. At his rebuke nations shall flee before him; and he shall reprove sinners for the thoughts of their heart. . . . And there shall be no unrighteousness in his days in their midst, for all shall be holy and their king the Lord Messiah.'

At Qumran, the title 'Messiah' was given not only to the expected Son of David but also to the future High Priest. But the commonest Messianic title in the Scrolls is 'Prince' (from Ezek. 34: 24; 37: 25).

In the first chapter of St John's gospel, 'Messiah' is only one of the titles given to Jesus by his earliest disciples. He forbade them to use it during his public ministry.

117

BIBLIOGRAPHY FOR FURTHER STUDY

Barrett, C. K., *The New Testament Background: Selected Documents*, London, 1956.

Bonsirven, J., *Le Judaisme palestinien au temps de Jésus Christ*, 2 vols., Paris, 1934.

Cross, F. M., *The Ancient Library of Qumran*, London, 1958.

Filson, F. V., *A New Testament History*, London, 1965.

Förster, W., *Palestinian Judaism in New Testament Times*, London, 1964.

Grant, F. C., *Ancient Judaism and the New Testament*, London, 1960.

Grant, F. C., *Roman Hellenism and the New Testament*, London, 1962.

Jeremias, J., *Jerusalem zur Zeit Jesu*, Ed. 3, Göttingen, 1962.

Lagrange, M. J., *Histoire ancienne du Nouveau Testament*, Paris, 1933.

Lagrange, M. J., *Le Judaisme avant Jésus Christ*, Ed. 2, Paris, 1931.

Moore, G. F., *Judaism in the First Centuries of the Christian Era*, 3 vols., Harvard, 1950.

Parkes, J., *The Foundations of Judaism and Christianity*, London, 1960.

Perowne, S., *The Life and Times of Herod the Great*, London, 1956.

Sherwin-Whyte, A. N., *Roman Society and Roman Law in the New Testament*, Oxford, 1963.

Stevenson, J., *A New Eusebius* (Documents illustrative of the history of the Church to A.D. 336), London, 1957.

Sutcliffe, E., *The Monks of Qumran*, London, 1960.

Williamson, G. A., *Eusebius: History of the Church from Christ to Constantine*, Harmondsworth (Penguin Classics), 1965.

INDEX